How To Identify High-Profit Elliott Wave Trades in Real Time

How To Identify High-Profit Elliott Wave Trades in Real Time

Pinpointing Optimal Entry/Exit Points with the C Wave Method

Myles Wilson Walker

© 1996 by Myles Wilson Walker

Published by Windsor Books
P.O. Box 280
Brightwaters, NY 11718

Printed in the United States of America

ISBN 0-930233-57-3

About the Author

Myles Wilson Walker has been trading full time since 1986 for himself and others. Initially skeptical about the value of Elliott Wave Principles, Mr. Walker conducted an intense study of all available literature. His goal was to distill the essential elements of Elliott's wave theory, then structure a successful trading program around them that was tradable in real time. This Mr. Walker accomplished, initially using the 24-hour currency markets as his main trading medium, then expanding the analysis to incorporate virtually all major markets. The results of this research are presented here in Mr. Walker's first book.

Mr. Walker was born in Auckland, New Zealand, where he currently resides.

Contents

Introduction

As a novice student, you would not expect to grasp the difficult concepts of Elliott's Wave Principle instantly. Understanding and successfully using this methodology for analyzing market price movements takes practice and perseverance.

In essence, the Elliott Wave Principle maintains that markets advance or decline in a series of wave patterns—five waves in the direction of the major trend and three waves in the direction of the correction of the major trend. This book is structured to help you broaden your knowledge base of Elliott's wave analysis step-by-step. I suggest that your first reading be a quick scan of all the material to give you an initial overview. Then, as you go back and study the concepts, which are explained in numerous and subtly different ways, you will find an approach that makes sense to you.

This book is essentially different from previous books on Elliott Wave in that I have attempted to quantify aspects of the theory into practical and workable guidelines with specific Buy and Sell patterns. There is no longer any guesswork. You will be able to match the C wave patterns as they are happening in real time and execute the trade according to established rules.

One reason I wanted to publish this book was to provide other traders with reliable Elliott Wave-based strategies rather than a rehash of Elliott Wave theory. Thus, I have kept certain aspects of the theory to a minimum and presented the material that I know from experience works. Until I can distill reliable rules, I feel that it would be unfair to present other information as the truth when in fact it still requires further research.

The first chapters of this book, which deal with Elliott Wave basics, will teach you the concepts and help you understand the C wave patterns. These C wave patterns are complete within themselves and stand alone without any other technical indicators or other market inputs.

Basics of Counting Waves

Imagine a wave of water: It is made up of droplets. The momentum of the water flow has picked up the droplets and unified them in the same direction. Between each wave is a trough of inactivity that sometimes runs counter as an undercurrent. Waves of market activity behave much the same as waves of water. At one moment all is quiet; then some new information hits the market and everyone is active, the wave picks up and continues until it can no longer be sustained. Then the market goes sideways through lack of activity or countertrend (the wave trough) because of profit taking.

This ebb and flow of market activity represents the price waves that Ralph Nelson Elliott categorized in his theory on market behavior during his pioneering work of the late 1920s through the 1940s.

Simply, a wave is seen as one constant direction in prices until it either stops and goes sideways or the direction totally changes.

This wave (wave 1) is an upward moving wave.

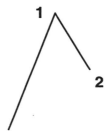

The next wave (wave 2) goes in the opposite direction. In this case, wave 2 is going down.

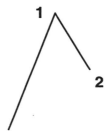

If you could see more detail of wave 1, you would see that it is made up of smaller waves—in this case five.

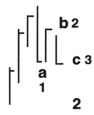

Wave 2 consists of three smaller waves. When any wave is made up of three smaller waves, each wave is given a letter, in this case a = 1, b = 2, c = 3.

Or wave 1 could be made up of only three smaller waves. If the wave consists of only three waves, it is marked as wave A or wave a.

If wave 1 were made up of only three waves, then wave 2 would always be marked as wave B or wave b.

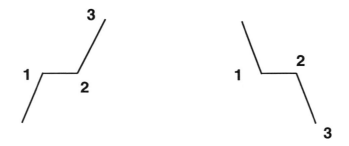

In this instance, the second wave is going sideways. A sideways price area is a wave and must be counted.

If you could see more detail of the sideways price movement, you could see that it is made up of smaller waves.

Wave 3 is made up of five smaller waves.

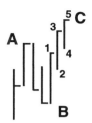

Wave B ends, and wave C follows. Wave C usually consists of five waves.

Wave 4 is made up of three waves (the same as wave 2).

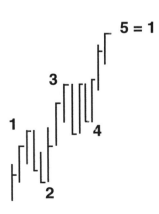

When wave 5 ends, the waves are then counted as one wave. At this stage, a movement (market correction) opposite the trend is expected.

Midpoint Method of Wave Counting

Another way of counting waves, called the *midpoint method*, is to smooth the daily data by using only the middle of the day's range. This method gives only one point of data a day, which makes it easier to see possible waves.

The main drawback of the midpoint method is that it is not sensitive enough to detect all the details of a C wave. However, when used in combination with detailed daily charts, this method can be useful in offering fresh insight to a muddled trading situation.

Midpoint

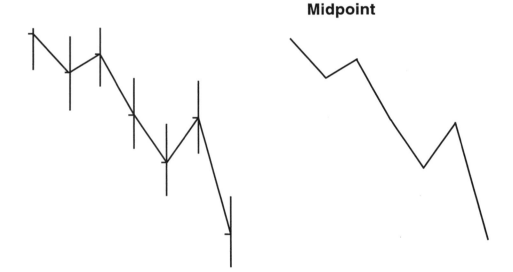

A single line connects the middle of each day's range.

Elliott Wave Principles

According to Elliott Wave Theory, the market unfolds according to a basic pattern of five waves up and three waves down to form a complete cycle of eight waves. The five waves up, called *impulsive* waves, occur in the direction of the trend. The three waves down, called *corrective* waves, are a price reaction against the trend. A sideways market is also considered corrective.

Most market analysis is concerned with the 80 percent of the time that the market is in a corrective state.

Impulse Waves

An impulse wave is a movement in the direction of the major trend. An impulse wave must obey all the rules listed below (if it does not, the wave in question must be classified as a correction even if it is also moving in the direction of the major trend). Although this seems illogical at first, by applying the rules you will not mistake a running correction for an impulse.

Impulse Rules

The following rules apply to impulse waves:

- Wave 1, wave 3 and wave 5 are trending.
- Wave 2 and wave 4 are corrections.
- Of wave 1, wave 3 and wave 5, wave 3 must not be the shortest.
- Wave 2 can retrace up to 99 percent of wave 1.
- Wave 4 may not retrace all of wave 3.
- Wave 4 should not go into the price area of wave 2. (Sometimes it will pull back to the top of wave 1.)
- Wave 2 and wave 4 must display alternation in as many ways as possible.

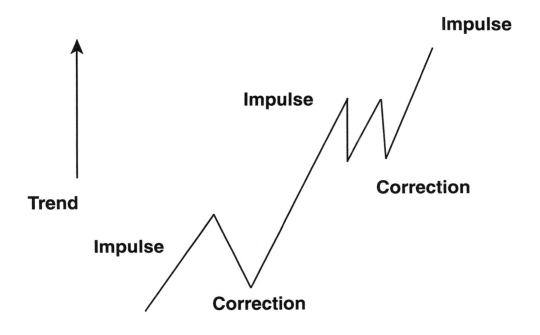

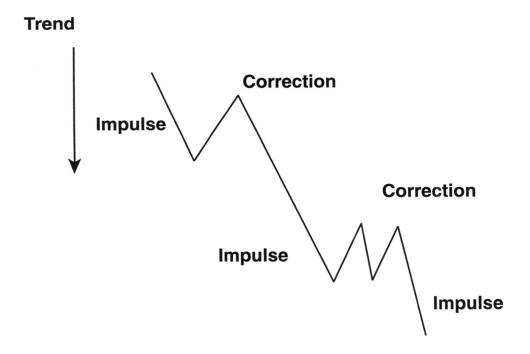

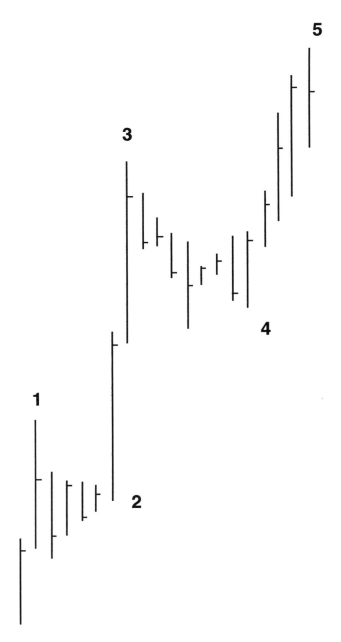

The structure of an impulse wave is illustrated here.

- Wave 1, wave 3 and wave 5 are trending.
- Wave 2 and wave 4 are corrections.
- Wave 4 does not go into the price area of wave 2.
- Of wave 1, wave 3 and wave 5, wave 3 is not the shortest.
- Wave 2 and wave 4 display alternation.

Counting Waves

When deciding if a wave fits into either an impulse or corrective framework, look for some basic visual things that will instantly show you the right category. These are illustrated by the following two diagrams.

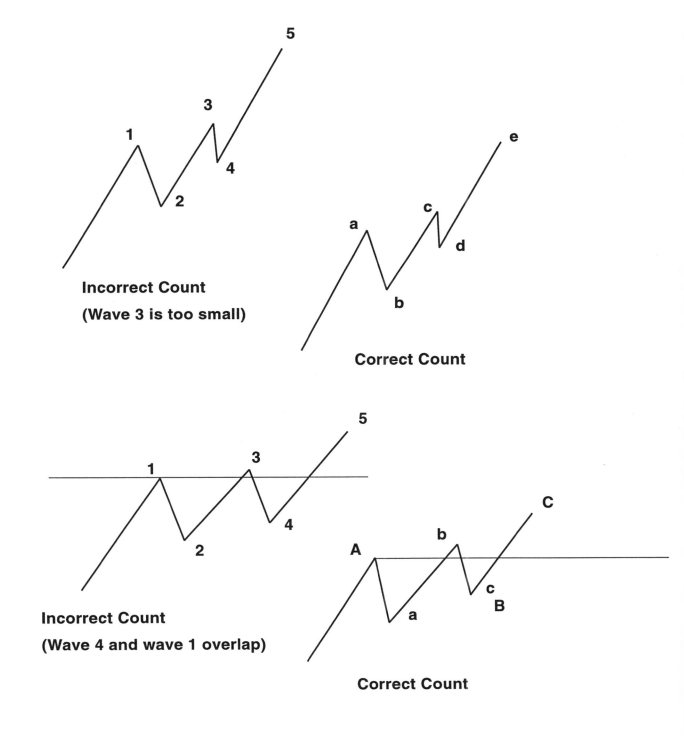

Alternation

In an impulse move, *alternation* must occur between wave 2 and wave 4. That is, wave 2 and wave 4 must be different in as many ways as possible, or at a minimum in at least one way.

Alternation occurs between wave 2 and wave 4 as either price, time or pattern type.

- *Price*: Wave 2 when compared to wave 4 may be obviously smaller/larger in price.

- *Time*: Wave 2 when compared to wave 4 may take much more/less time.

- *Pattern*: Wave 2 may be a simple A B C. Wave 4 could be a more complex A B C or even a fourth wave triangle. Wave 2 could be a flat. Wave 4 could be a zigzag or vice versa.

The following diagrams illustrate various forms of alternation.

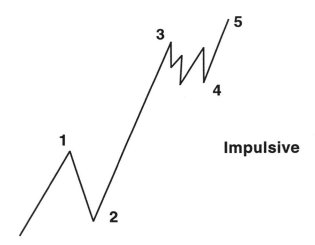

In this diagram, there is alternation between wave 2 and wave 4 in both price and pattern. Wave 2 retraces more of wave 1 than wave 4 retraces wave 3.

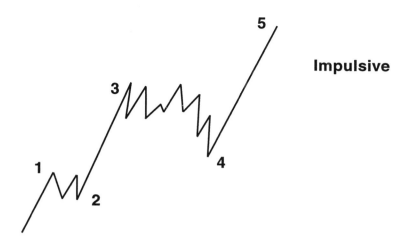

Impulsive

In this diagram, wave 2 and wave 4 display alternation in price, pattern and time.

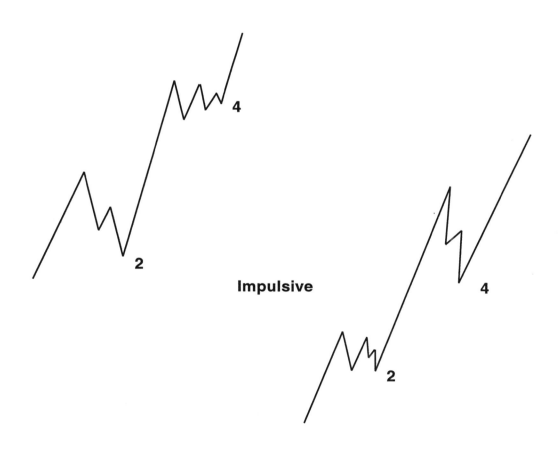

Impulsive

For a pattern to be impulsive, wave 2 and wave 4 must be noticeably different.

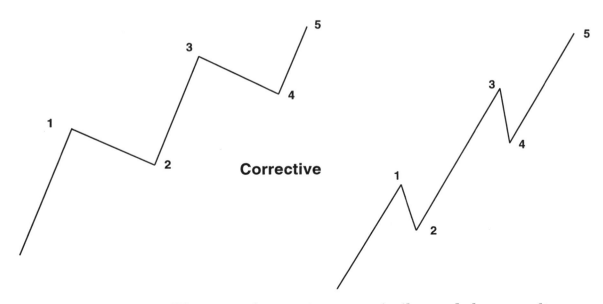

Wave 2 and wave 4 are too similar and show no alternation. The complete wave sequence is corrective.

Degree

The waves on a monthly chart are much larger than those found on an intraday chart comprised of two-hour time frames. If you study a price chart, the *degree* of each wave is easily recognized. You can easily see that some waves consume more time and price than others.

When dealing with small time frames, it is essential to group all the smaller waves into bigger ones. The waves on a five-minute chart are grouped to make up an hourly chart. The hourly chart is then grouped to make up a daily chart. The daily is then grouped to make up a monthly chart and so on. The data on a five-minute chart is of minor importance when viewed historically as compared to the data on a monthly chart, thus the five-minute chart is said to be of much smaller degree than the monthly.

To count waves properly, it is essential to group the waves of the same degree together. This can be difficult since each wave can expand in time or extend in price and still be of the same degree. Corrections are notorious for this, and it is easy to get lost in the count until the correction is over, especially when you are dealing in small time frames.

Monthly Cash S&P 500

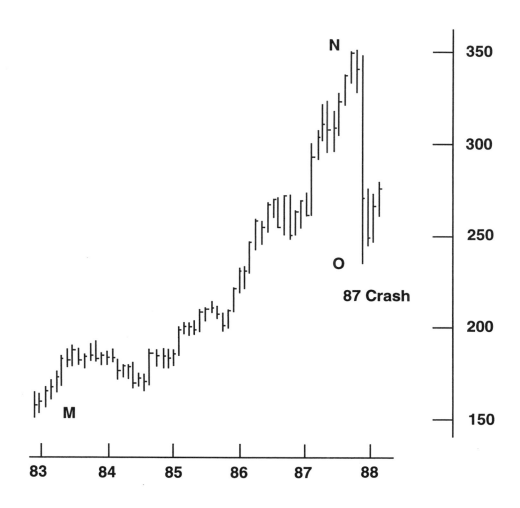

The rally from M to N was the same wave degree as the 1987 crash N to O.

The S&P chart on the following page shows that C wave patterns can be found on waves of the smallest degree possible.

S&P 500 1 Minute

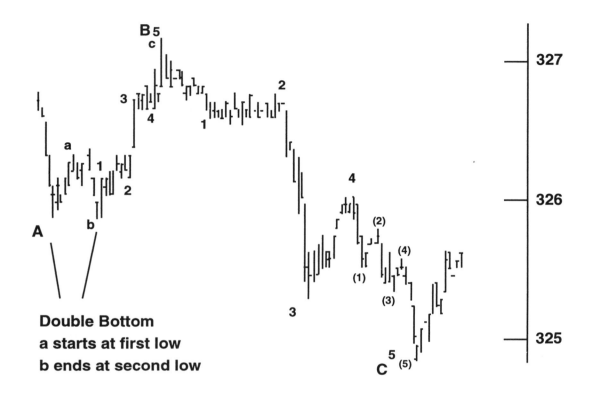

Double Bottom

a starts at first low

b ends at second low

Extensions

When you look at a price chart and compare the three impulse waves, you will notice that one of them is longer than the rest. This longer wave is said to be *extended*.

Waves extend because of market psychology. Traders recognize the trend and at the point it becomes a common perception, the market starts to stretch. Very little counter-trend action occurs since most players are waiting for reactions to join in or add to positions.

During an extended wave, incredible amounts of price distance can be covered with very little in the way of a pullback. The great danger here is that even if you are personally sure that the market is trending, you will not know which wave is extending until well into the move. To prevent premature profit-taking on position trades, you must be aware of the concept of the extended wave.

The diagram below demonstrates the concept that an impulse sequence contains one wave that is noticeably longer than the others.

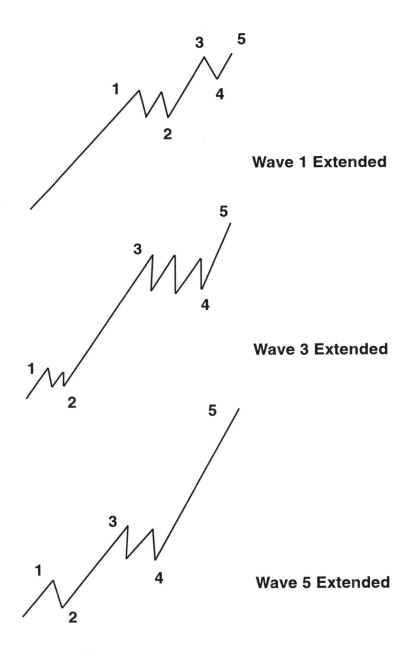

Wave 1 Extended

Wave 3 Extended

Wave 5 Extended

Corrective Waves

Corrective waves are comprised of three waves. Corrections move in the opposite direction to the main trend. Therefore, the first wave (wave A) will be the reverse of the trend. The second wave (wave B) will be in the direction of the trend. The last wave (wave C) will be against the trend. Wave A and wave B may be comprised of five waves of one smaller degree.

A B C Corrections

A B C corrections are the most common corrective structures with five wave triangles following. As a trader, you are always looking for wave C to complete, so that you can re-enter the market in the direction of the main trend.

These diagrams illustrate simple A B C corrections.

ESSENCE →

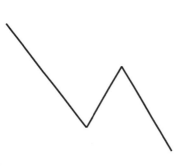

Zigzag

Zigzag

Flat

Flat

The more time the correction takes, the more complex the wave needs to become.

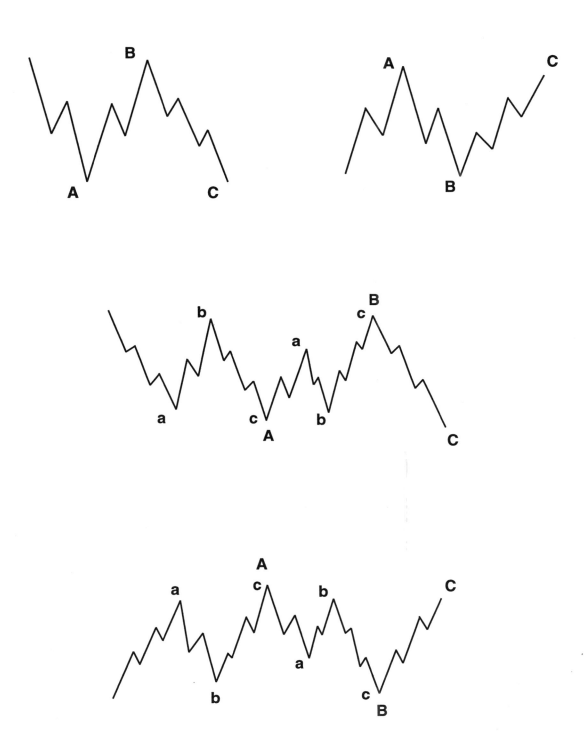

C waves can take up a lot of time and also cover a lot of price distance. They do this by having smaller and smaller subwaves.

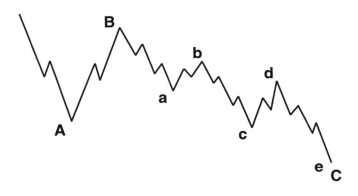

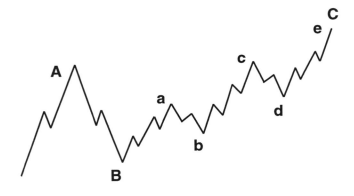

Zigzags

A *zigzag* is a corrective wave that divides into a three wave (A B C) sequence. If a zigzag subdivides:

- Wave A is made of 5 waves.
- Wave B is made of 3 waves.
- Wave C is made of 5 waves.

Sometimes a zigzag is simple, as illustrated in the following diagrams. All zigzags obey the following essential rules:

- Wave B may not retrace more than 61.8 percent of wave A.
- Wave C must retrace all of wave B.

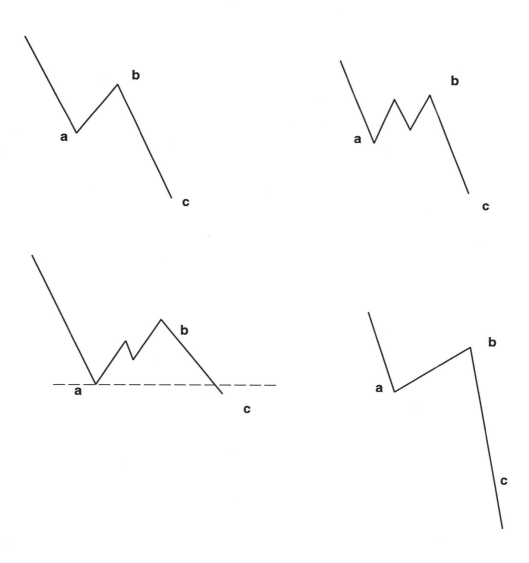

Deutschemark U.S. Spot Daily

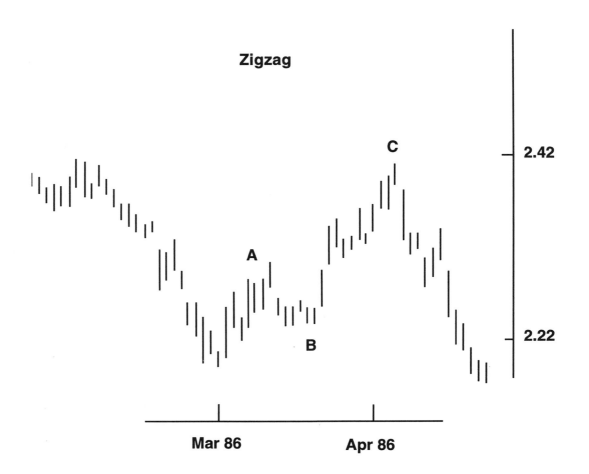

Flats

The term *flat* refers to any A B C correction that obeys the following essential rules:

- Wave B must retrace more than 61.8 percent of wave A.

- Wave C must be at least 38.2 percent of wave B.

- Wave B can be 61.8 percent to 138.2 percent of wave A.

162 ?

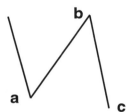

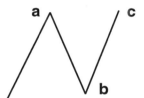

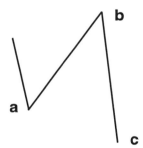

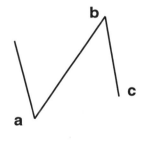

Elongated Flats

Elongated flats often form complete corrections. Occasionally, they form part of a larger triangle.

Rule: Wave C must be a minimum length of 138.20 percent when compared to wave B.

Often wave C will be 161.8 percent to 238.20 percent of wave B.

Wave C will often consume the most amount of time when compared to wave A and wave B.

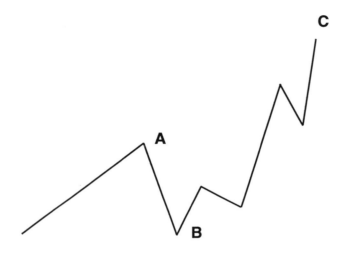

Deutschemark U.S. Spot Daily

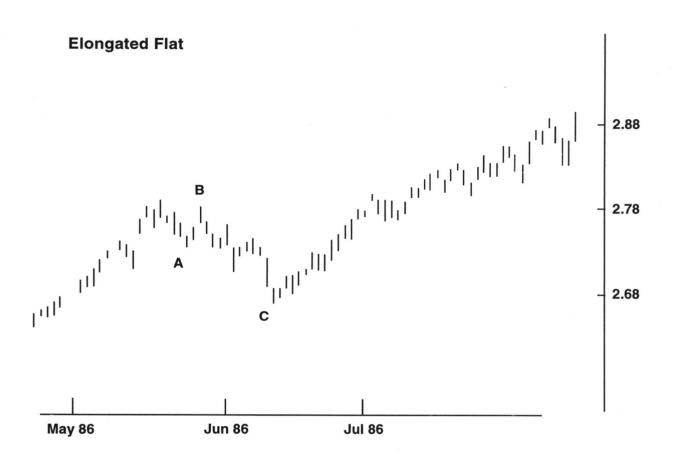

Elongated Flat

Triangles

Normal *triangles* consist of five wave corrections that often occur in the fourth wave and B wave position. Each of the five waves usually subdivides into three waves. If you believe that you are in a fourth wave triangle, expect to see multiple subdivisions into threes and a lot of time elapse compared to previous waves (often months on daily). The market will make false trendline breaks as it tends to drift sideways. This is a characteristic of B and fourth wave triangles.

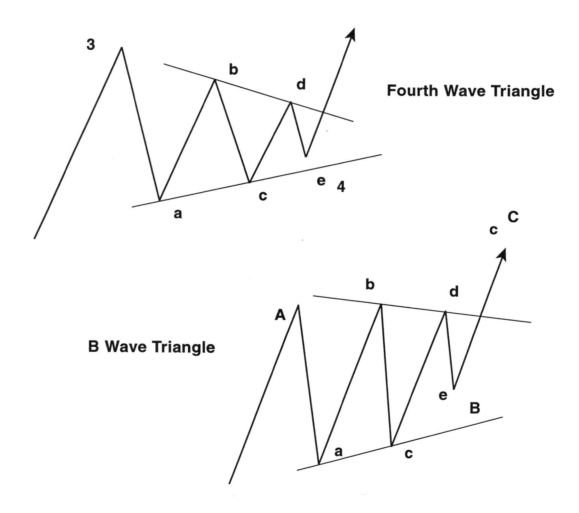

Triangles consist of five corrective waves labeled a b c d e. Once the market has broken the b d trendline, the triangle is complete.

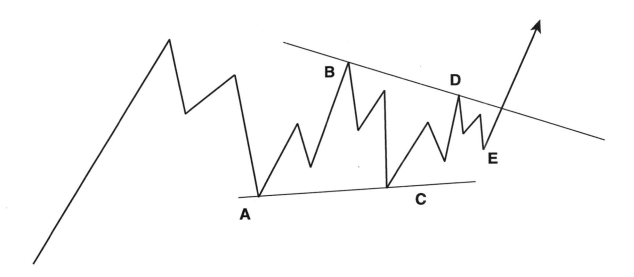

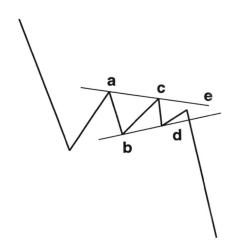

Each wave of a triangle may or may not subdivide. The five wave structure and general shape makes it obvious that a triangle has formed.

Diagonal Triangles

Diagonal triangles consist of five waves and can occur at the end of any movement that needs five waves to complete (e.g., a wave C or a wave 5 of a fifth wave of one larger degree). When you see a diagonal triangle as the last wave of a wave 5, expect a major move to follow.

One of the most important patterns, diagonal triangles are discussed in greater detail in Chapter 5. Diagonal triangles can be found on charts of all degree. The psychology behind the pattern is this: People are still trying to buy at the top but are meeting with selling resistance; and when the diagonal triangle is forming at a bottom, people are still trying to sell but are meeting with buying support. The result is an overlapping of wave b, wave c, wave d and wave e.

Sometimes when you look at the wave, you will see that some waves are simple. For instance, wave B might be very simple whereas wave C could subdivide into five waves. The most unlikely place for a multiple subdivision of waves is wave D. The key to the diagonal five wave triangle is having a clear B D trendline. If the B D trendline is not obvious, more work needs to be done within the triangle.

Deutschemark U.S. Spot Daily

Fifth Wave Triangle

1985 Top on U.S. Dollar

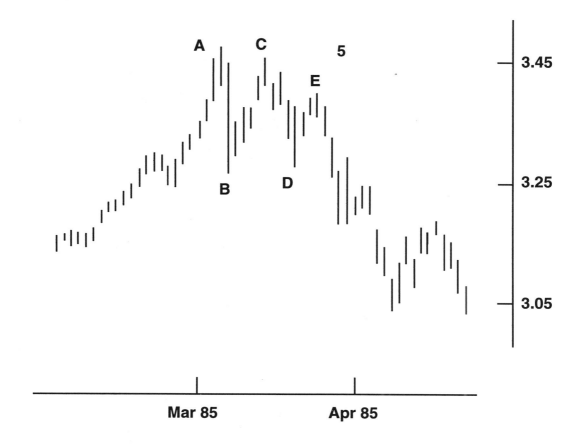

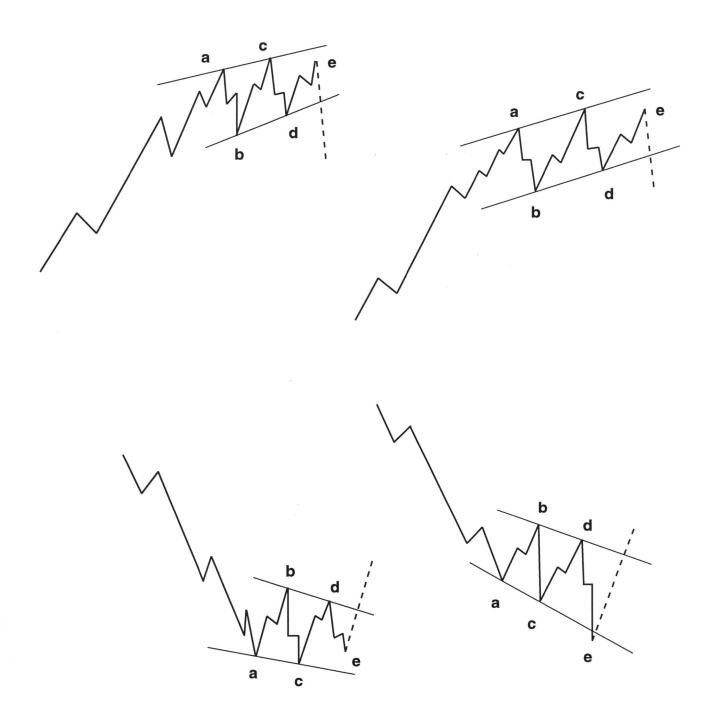

Five wave (diagonal) triangles can complete any move that needs five waves to complete, such as wave C or a fifth wave of any degree.

Running Corrections

A *running correction* corrects in the direction of the trend. This is possibly the most difficult of all the wave concepts to grasp. Attention to detail is essential in recognizing a running correction.

If the market does not follow the rules of an impulse wave, it is corrective. It does not matter if the wave is going in the direction of the trend. A running correction indicates a very strong market. In the following illustration, wave a, wave b and wave c are part of the same correction. Strong B waves are covered in detail in Chapter 5.

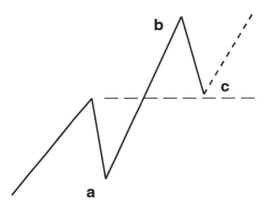

C Wave Failures

When wave C fails to retrace all of wave B, the complete A B C pattern will be classified as a *C wave failure*. The power implications of this pattern are dependent on the degree of the wave that is being dealt with. On daily charts, the move to follow will be strong.

C wave failures occur frequently on intraday charts but the follow-through is negligible.

Deutschemark U.S. Spot Daily

C Wave Failure

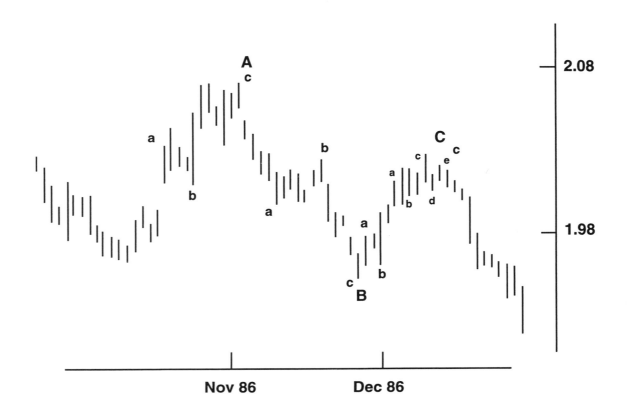

Fifth Wave Failures

On daily charts, *fifth wave failures* are relatively rare. However, this does not hold true on intraday charts. The move that follows a fifth wave failure is always powerful. The setup is easy to analyze because the market will show normal impulsive behavior. That is:

- wave 3 is not the shortest price pattern,

- there is good alternation between wave 2 and wave 4, and

- in the fifth wave, the subdivisions will appear to show real weakness of trend.

At this point, be prepared to enter with an order in the market. In every fifth wave failure that I have traded, I doubt if I would have gotten a reasonable fill if I had waited to phone in my order as soon as I saw the break. A fifth wave failure is the strongest signal that the trend has changed. Of course, the degree of wave that you are dealing with determines whether it is the start of a fundamental trend change or the beginning of a correction.

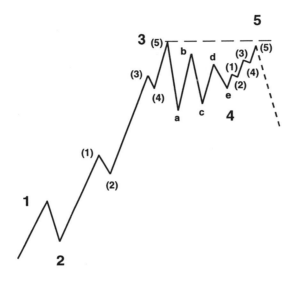

Wave 5 failed to make a new high. A fifth wave failure should be followed by a strong move in the opposite direction.

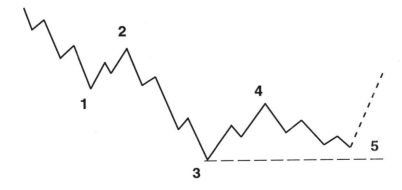

Wave 5 failed to make a new low. The upward move to follow should be strong.

3

Guidelines for Counting Waves

In Chapter 1, you looked at the basic concept of putting price flows into waves. When looking at price charts, you need a methodology to break the market movements into patterns of waves for later analysis. Start with big waves, then break these down into even smaller waves. Keep doing this until you have gone as far as you can with the type of charts that you are using (daily or different intraday periods). You will find the following guidelines helpful to the process of counting waves.

- Mark price extremes. This will be a group of waves.

- Break the groups of waves into even smaller groups, and apply impulse and correction rules to the smaller wave groups.

- Group similar adjacent waves.

- When the time frame that you are using becomes overcrowded, smooth the data by moving to the next highest time frame (e.g., 30 minutes to hourlies to two-hourlies to dailies to weeklies to monthlies).

- When the wave count becomes difficult, check a related market. This will often provide a clearer picture.

- Use a transparent overlay to trace over your charts. This way you can try different wave counts without spoiling your charts.

- When prices are congested in one area, look for an A B C pattern.

- At double bottoms, look for a C wave to follow the second low.

- When two areas of price congestion are linked by a simpler wave, the second congestion area is usually a C wave.

- Every price movement, no matter how small, is part of a wave and must be accounted for and identified in a logical way. To accommodate space restrictions and to leave charts uncluttered, you do not need to actually label every subwave. But no wave can be overlooked.

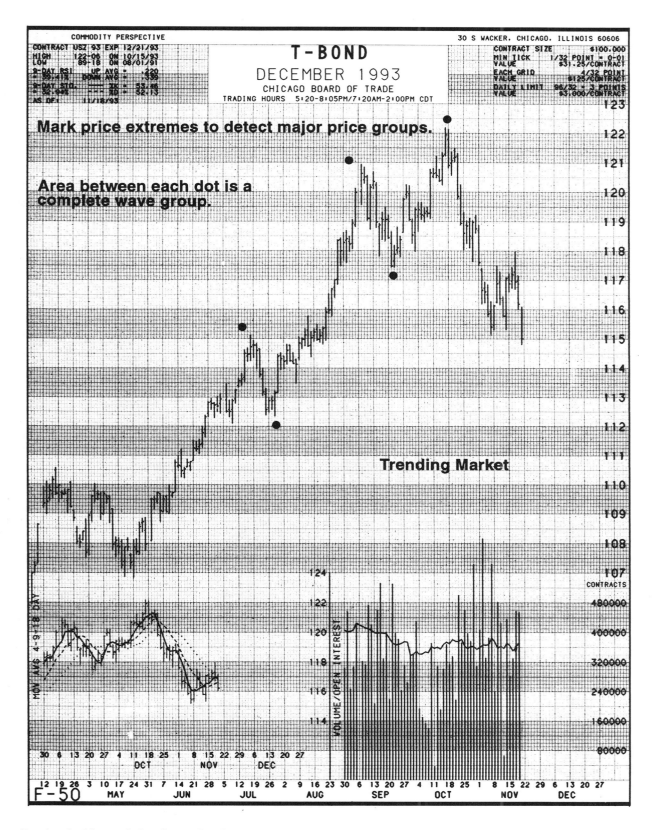

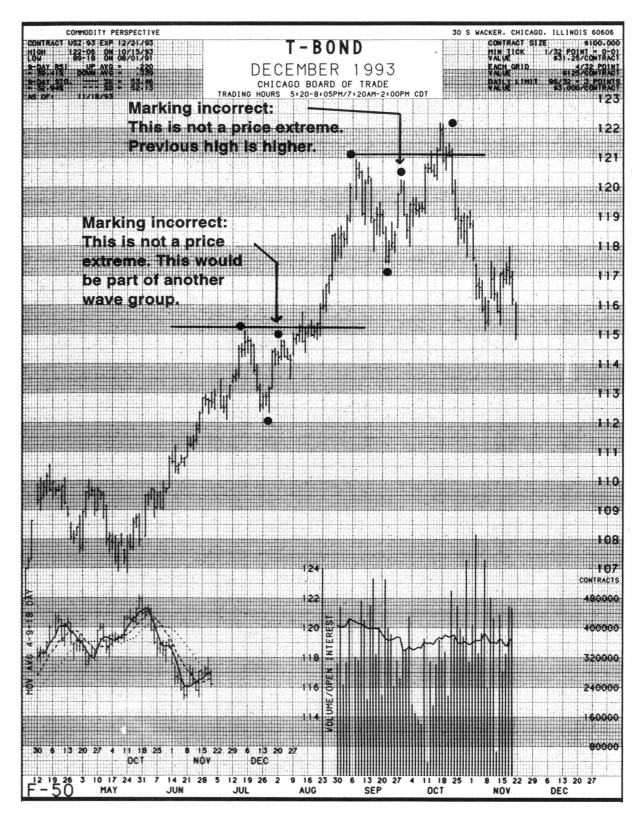

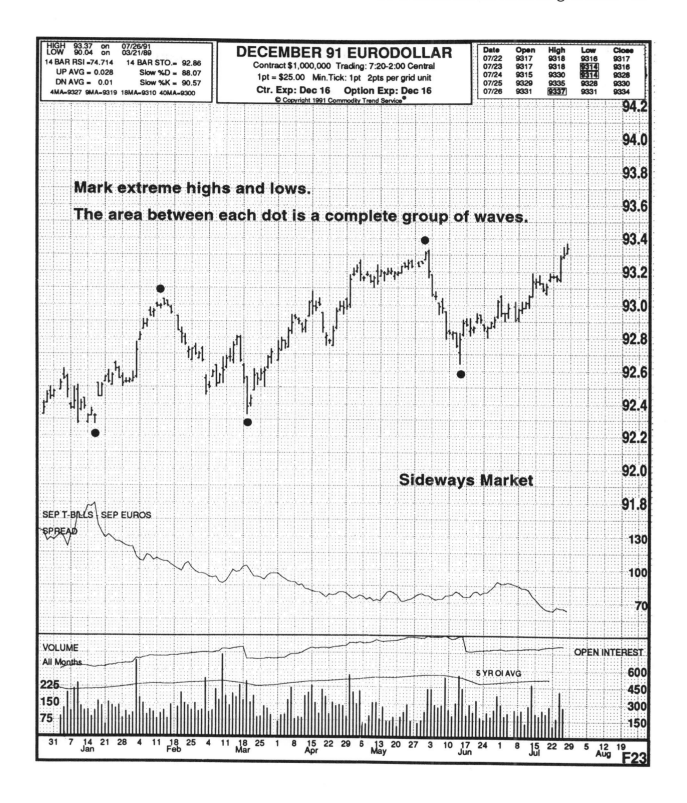

Reprinted with permission, © 1995 Commodity Trend Service

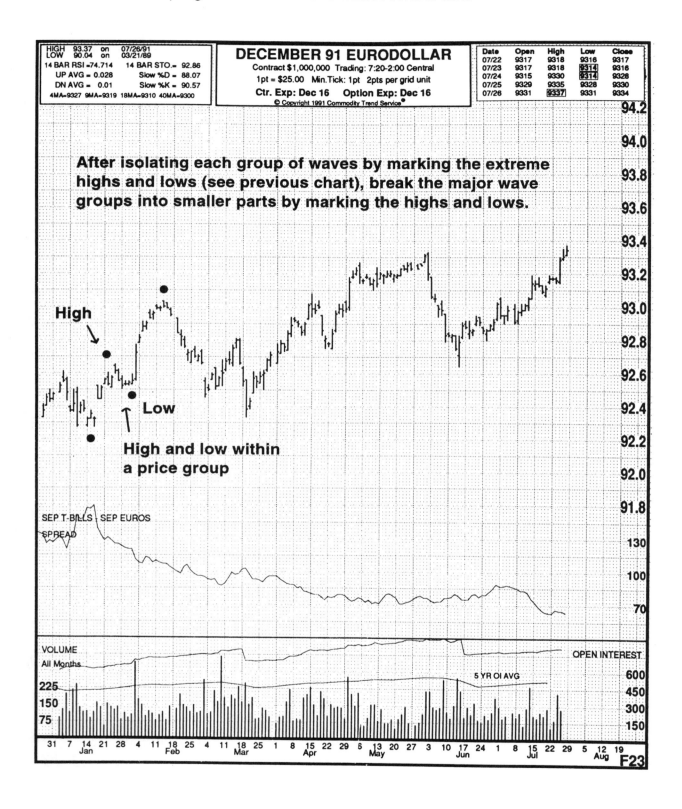

After isolating each group of waves by marking the extreme highs and lows (see previous chart), break the major wave groups into smaller parts by marking the highs and lows.

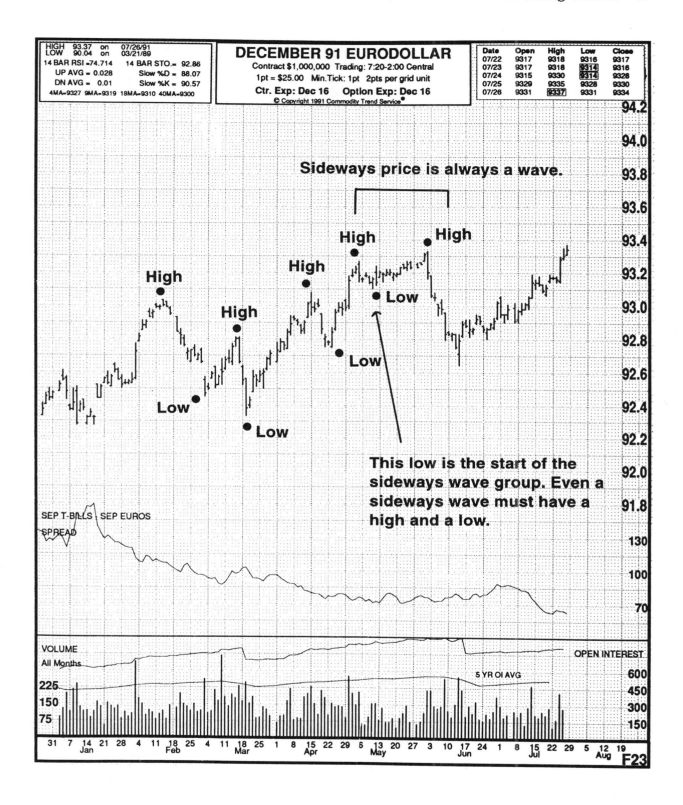

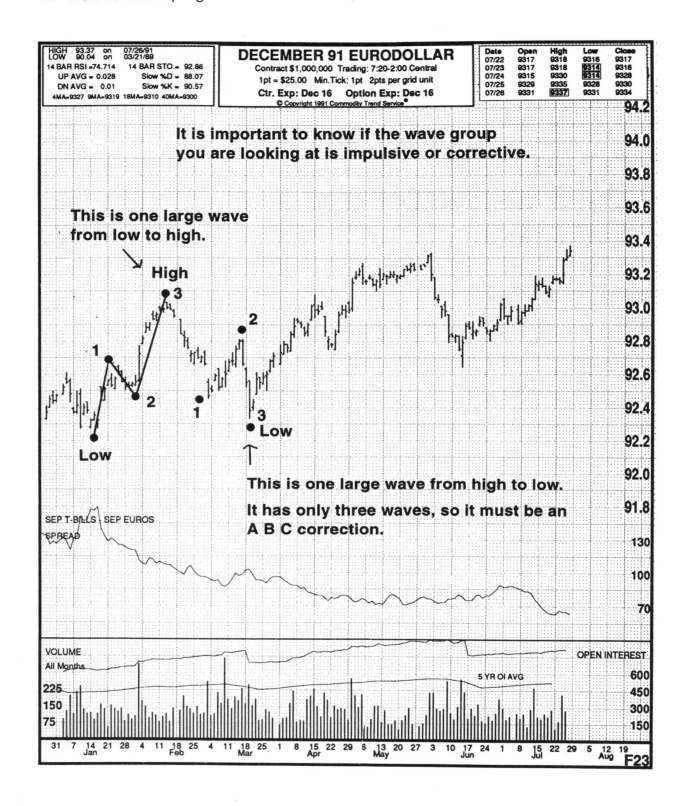

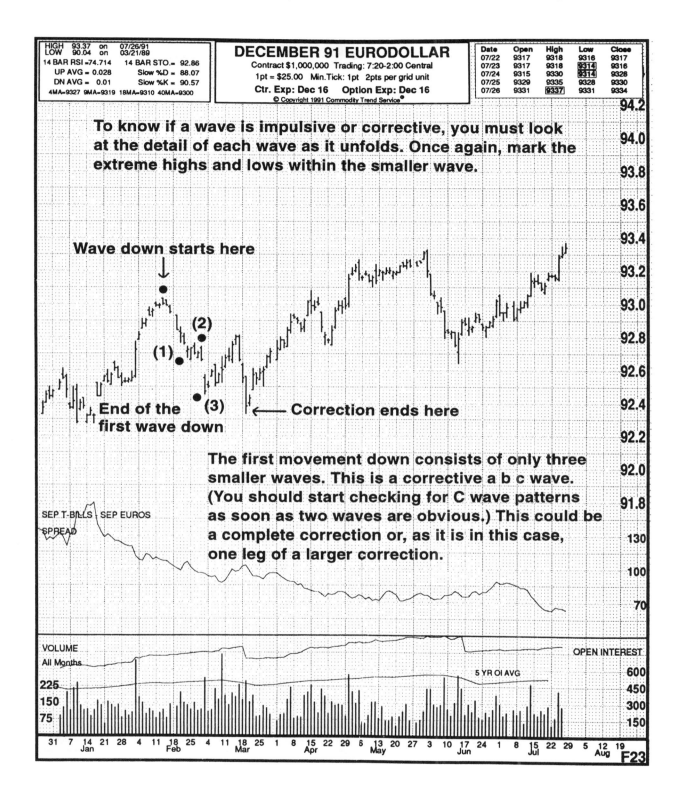

To know if a wave is impulsive or corrective, you must look at the detail of each wave as it unfolds. Once again, mark the extreme highs and lows within the smaller wave.

Wave down starts here

End of the first wave down

(1)

(2)

(3)

Correction ends here

The first movement down consists of only three smaller waves. This is a corrective a b c wave. (You should start checking for C wave patterns as soon as two waves are obvious.) This could be a complete correction or, as it is in this case, one leg of a larger correction.

DECEMBER 91 EURODOLLAR
Contract $1,000,000 Trading: 7:20-2:00 Central
1pt = $25.00 Min.Tick: 1pt 2pts per grid unit
Ctr. Exp: Dec 16   Option Exp: Dec 16
© Copyright 1991 Commodity Trend Service®

HIGH 93.37 on 07/26/91
LOW 90.04 on 03/21/89
14 BAR RSI =74.714   14 BAR STO.= 92.86
UP AVG = 0.028   Slow %D = 88.07
DN AVG = 0.01   Slow %K = 90.57
4MA=9327 9MA=9319 18MA=9310 40MA=9300

Date	Open	High	Low	Close
07/22	9317	9318	9316	9317
07/23	9317	9318	9314	9316
07/24	9315	9330	9314	9328
07/25	9329	9335	9328	9330
07/26	9331	9337	9331	9334

SEP T-BILLS \ SEP EUROS
SPREAD

VOLUME
All Months

OPEN INTEREST
5 YR OI AVG

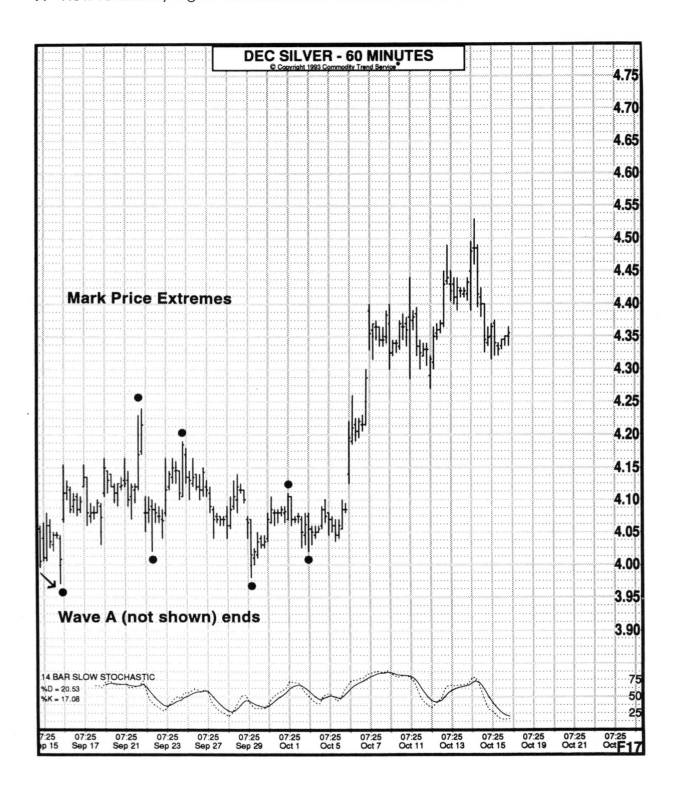

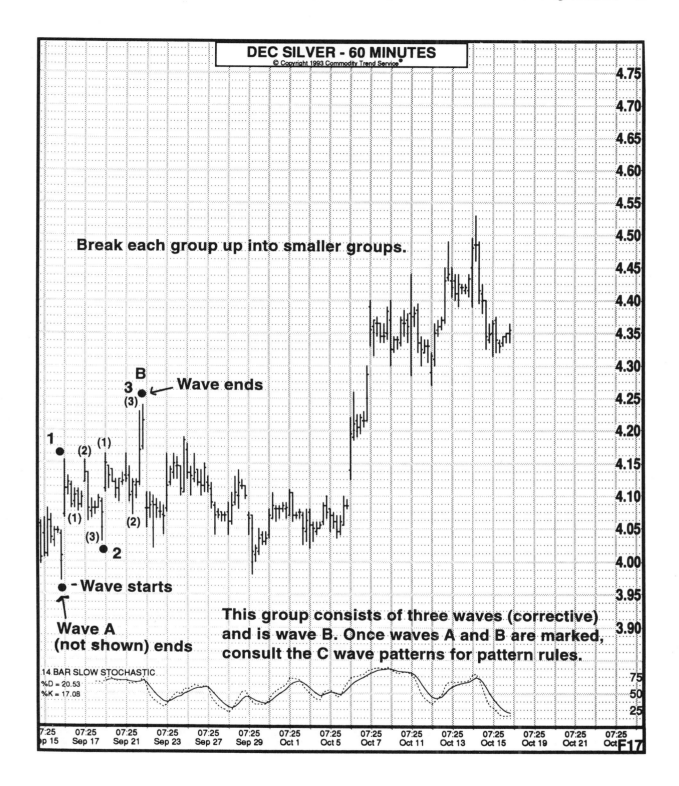

DEC SILVER - 60 MINUTES
© Copyright 1993 Commodity Trend Service

Break each group up into smaller groups.

B
3 ●← Wave ends
(3)

1 ● (2) (1)

(1)

(2)

(3)
● 2

● – Wave starts

Wave A
(not shown) ends

This group consists of three waves (corrective)
and is wave B. Once waves A and B are marked,
consult the C wave patterns for pattern rules.

14 BAR SLOW STOCHASTIC
%D = 20.53
%K = 17.08

7:25   07:25   07:25   07:25   07:25   07:25   07:25   07:25   07:25   07:25   07:25   07:25   07:25   07:25   07:25
p 15   Sep 17 Sep 21 Sep 23 Sep 27 Sep 29 Oct 1   Oct 5   Oct 7   Oct 11 Oct 13 Oct 15 Oct 19 Oct 21 Oct F17

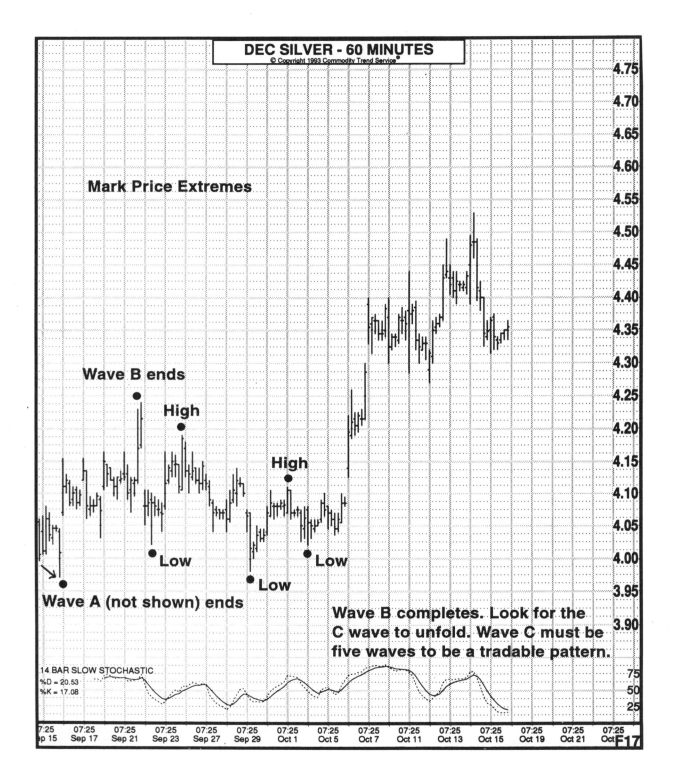

DEC SILVER - 60 MINUTES
© Copyright 1993 Commodity Trend Service

Mark Price Extremes

Wave B ends

High

High

Low

Low

Low

Wave A (not shown) ends

Wave B completes. Look for the
C wave to unfold. Wave C must be
five waves to be a tradable pattern.

14 BAR SLOW STOCHASTIC
%D = 20.53
%K = 17.08

Reprinted with permission, © 1995 Commodity Trend Service

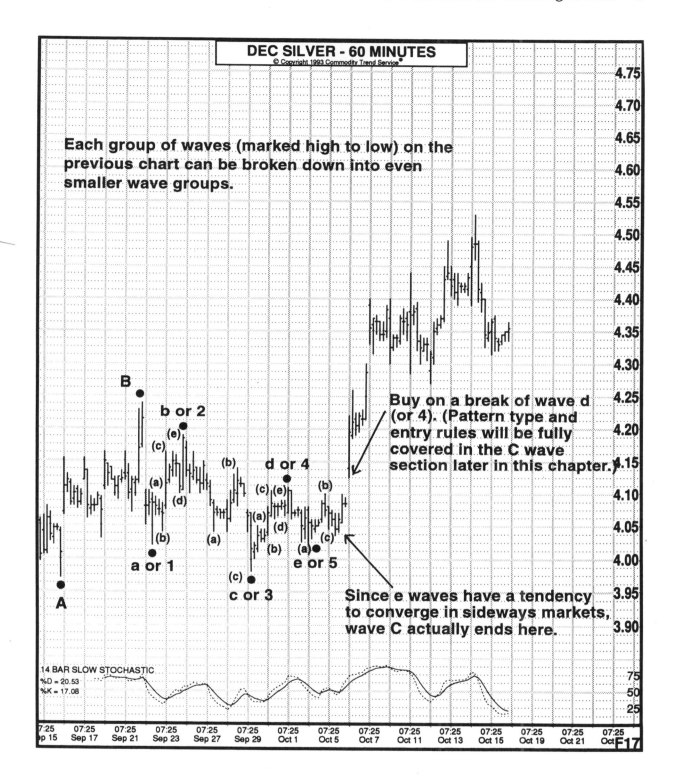

DEC SILVER - 60 MINUTES
© Copyright 1993 Commodity Trend Service®

Each group of waves (marked high to low) on the previous chart can be broken down into even smaller wave groups.

Buy on a break of wave d (or 4). (Pattern type and entry rules will be fully covered in the C wave section later in this chapter.)

Since e waves have a tendency to converge in sideways markets, wave C actually ends here.

14 BAR SLOW STOCHASTIC
%D = 20.53
%K = 17.08

Counting Waves

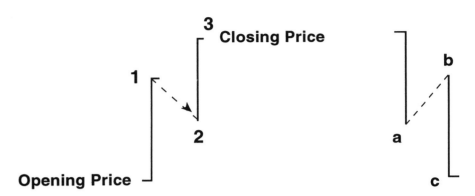

The overlapping on charts of any time frame is a wave.

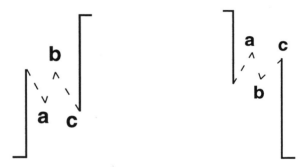

The overlapping on daily charts are small intraday corrections.

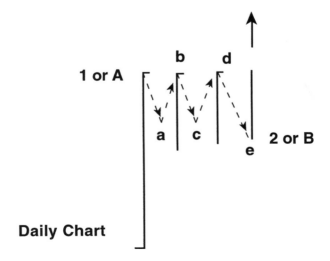

Use the previous day's close and today's high/low to determine wave flows.

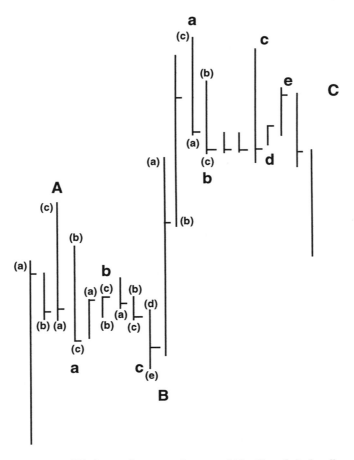

Using close prices with the highs/lows gives a good indication of market action during each time period.

Even though wave B is only one bar, when compared to surrounding price bars, it is significantly larger. Therefore, it is classified as a complete wave of one higher degree (i.e., B is the same price degree as all of A).

Grouping Similar Waves

The following waves look normal (of the same degree) because they are similar in either/or price and time. Waves must look like this to be considered part of the same group for counting purposes.

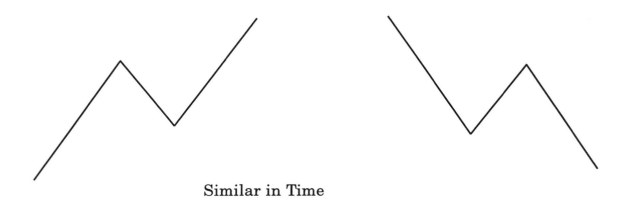

Similar in Time

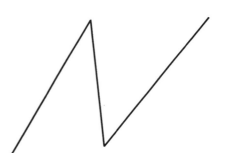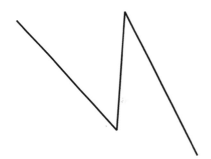

Similar in Price

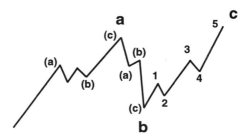

Smaller wave groups make up each leg of the a b c.

Detecting Elliott Wave Patterns and C Wave Patterns

Candlesticks are Best

actually p+f can be helpful at times

The only charts suitable for detecting Elliott Wave patterns and C wave patterns are *bar charts* with the high/low and close. A *line chart* that only displays one price per time period does not have enough sensitivity to show all the waves but can be useful for making an initial assessment. A *point and figure chart* does not account for time at all and for this reason cannot be used in any circumstances.

A bar chart can be displayed in time frames from one minute up to one year. Every market will have an optimum time frame that will best display the C wave patterns. Discovering the best time frame is a matter of researching individual markets.

Examples of various time frames are illustrated in Chapter 9. When trading, it is important to note that if you are taking trades on charts based on very small time frames, your profit will normally be much smaller than targets based on analysis from daily charts.

Terms

To help define patterns of waves, I find certain terms useful. Following is a list of terms with an explanation of their exact meaning.

Overlapping

When a wave returns into the price range of one (or more) previous waves, *overlapping* occurs.

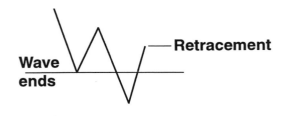

Wave 4 retraces past the end of wave 1.

Overlapping price retraces past the end of another complete wave.

Converging

Converging occurs when the wave group is comprised of shorter and smaller moves and can be contained by two trendlines that meet at a point. This pattern is found at the end of a larger wave group (i.e., wave e of a triangle, thus making a smaller triangle at the end of a triangle).

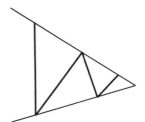
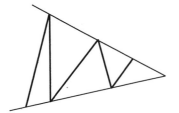

Subdivide

Market prices stretch by having complete but smaller, or *subdivided*, wave groups within a wave.

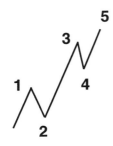

No waves subdivided

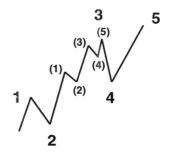

Wave 3 subdivided

Symbols of Wave Degree

Yes it is!

There are so many waves within waves that symbols must be used to denote which wave you are referring to. The focus of this book is the practical application of Elliott Wave Principles on a day-to-day basis. Thus, I have concentrated on a basic, simple explanation of the wave theory. On the charts, group the same-size letters or numbers with each other. A large A B C is of a higher degree than A B C, which is one level higher than a b c. Parentheses are used for the next degree down [e.g., (a) (b) (c)].

When dealing with C waves, the letters a, b, c, d, e are used interchangeably with the numbers 1, 2, 3, 4, 5. Therefore, a = 1, b = 2, c = 3, d = 4, e = 5. Thus, a break above wave 4 also means a break above wave d.

4

Logic of Counting Waves

The following group of charts will demonstrate a number of points pertaining to wave count logic. At any time when counting waves, a decision must be made as to whether a particular count is the best one possible. The points illustrated on the following charts are not iron-clad rules, but they will help you to decide which is the best possible count at the time.

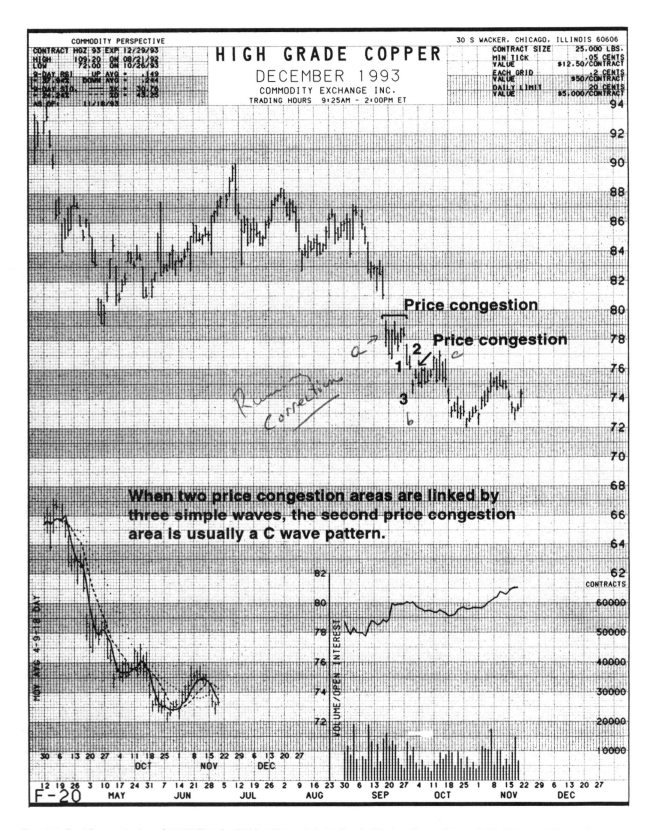

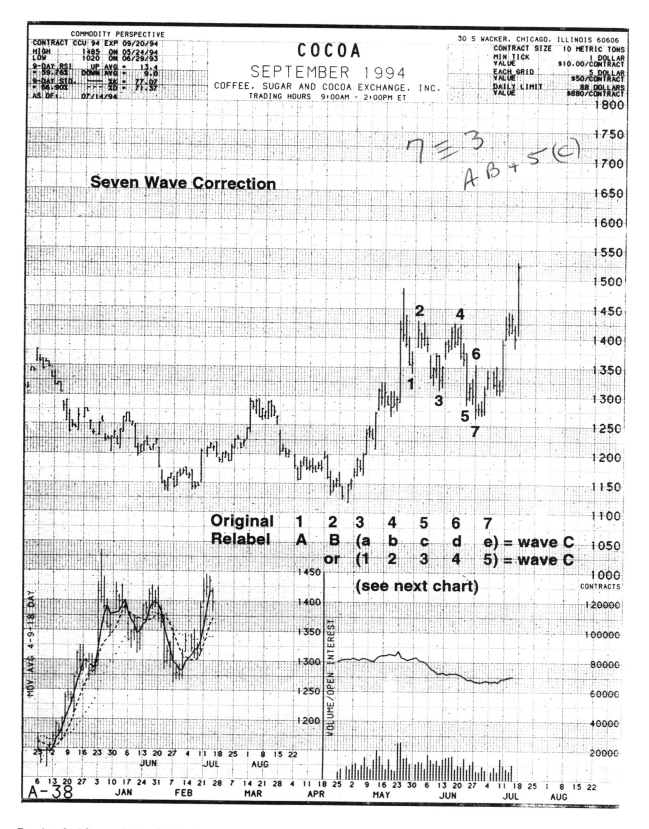

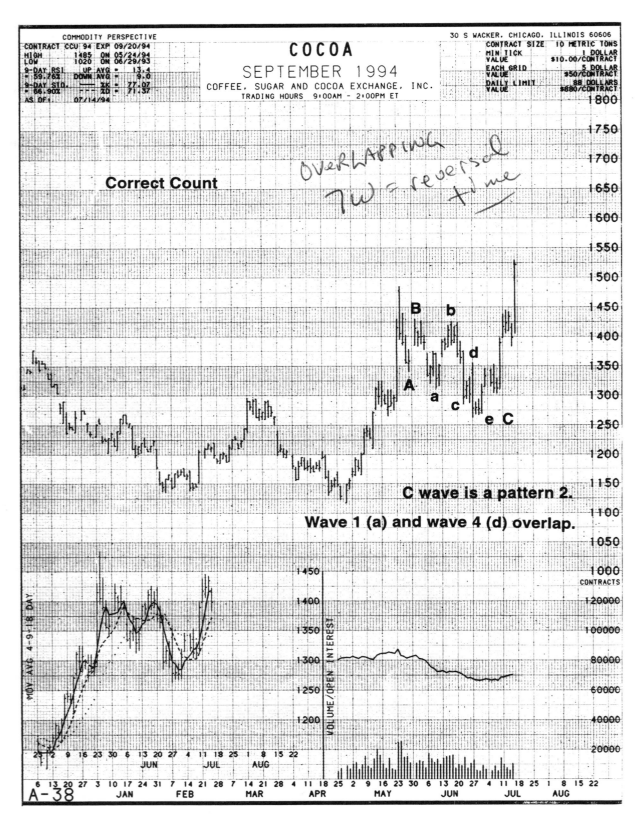

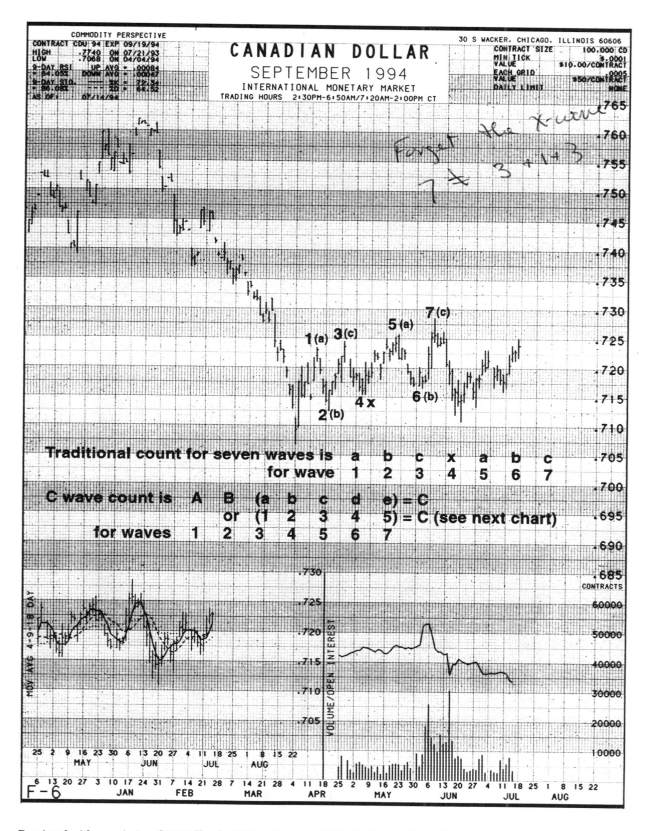

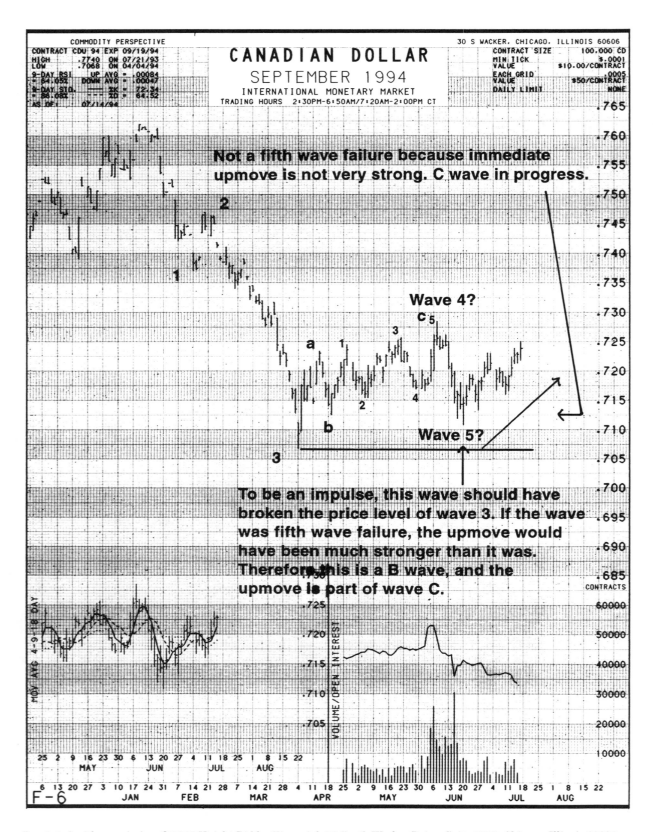

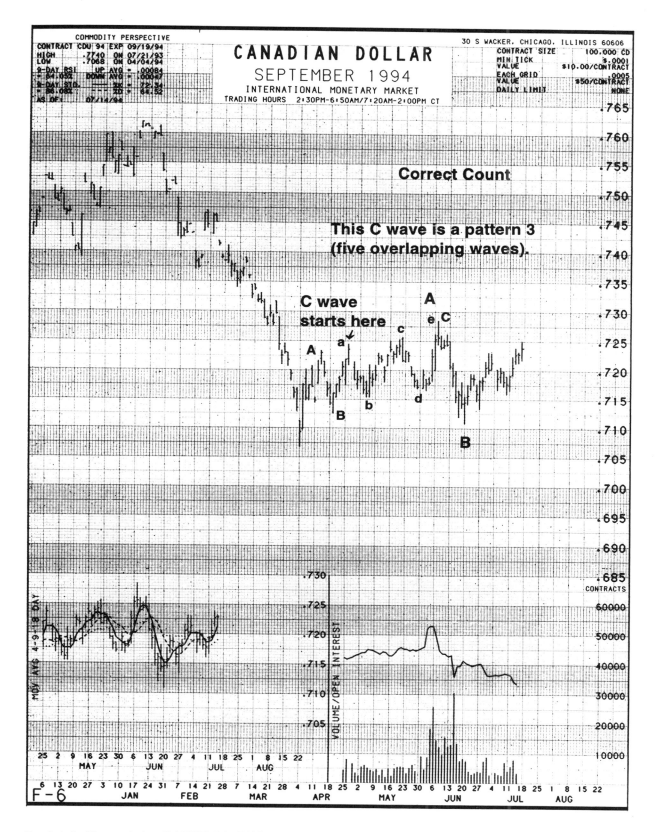

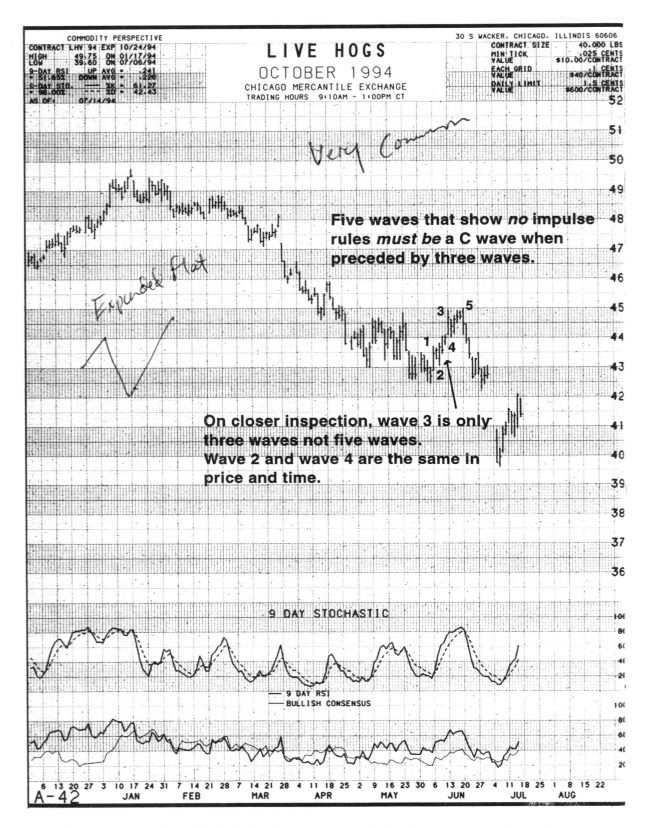

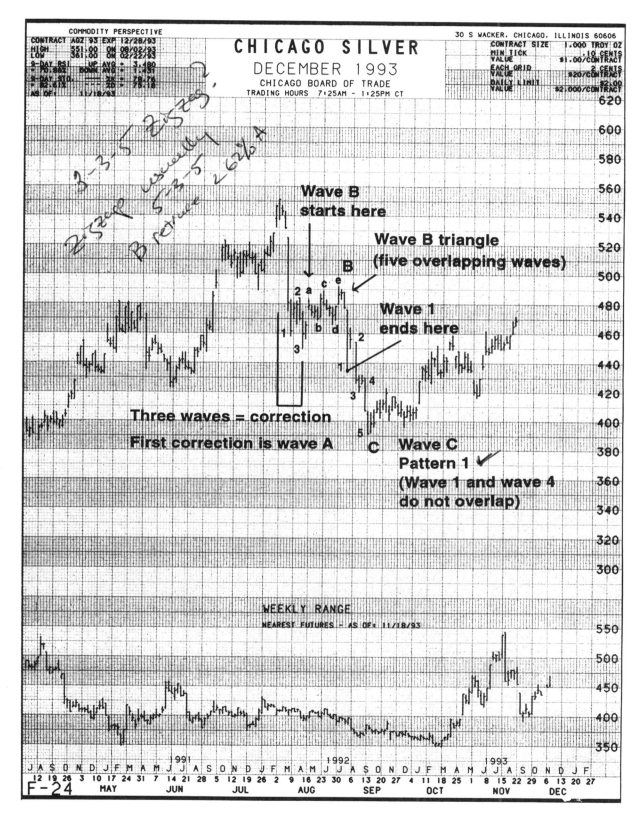

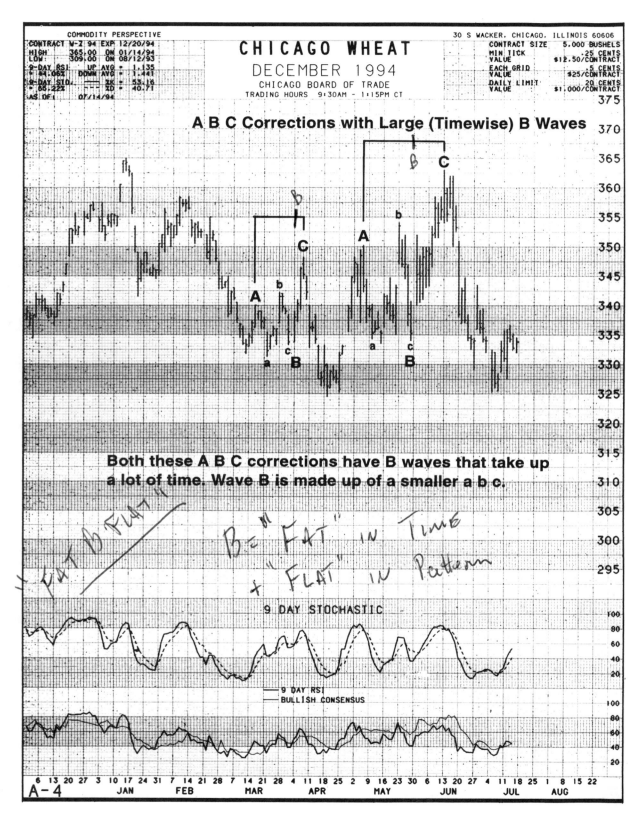

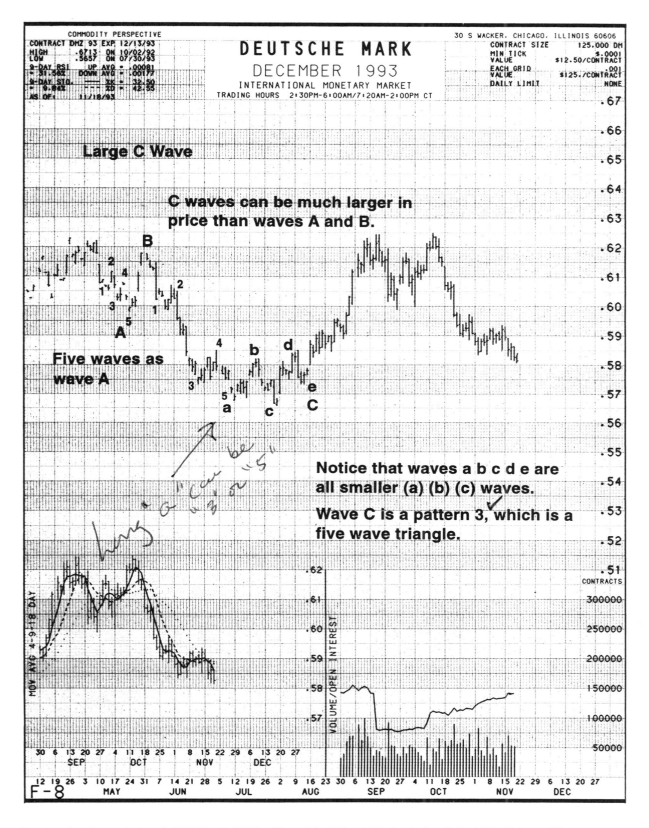

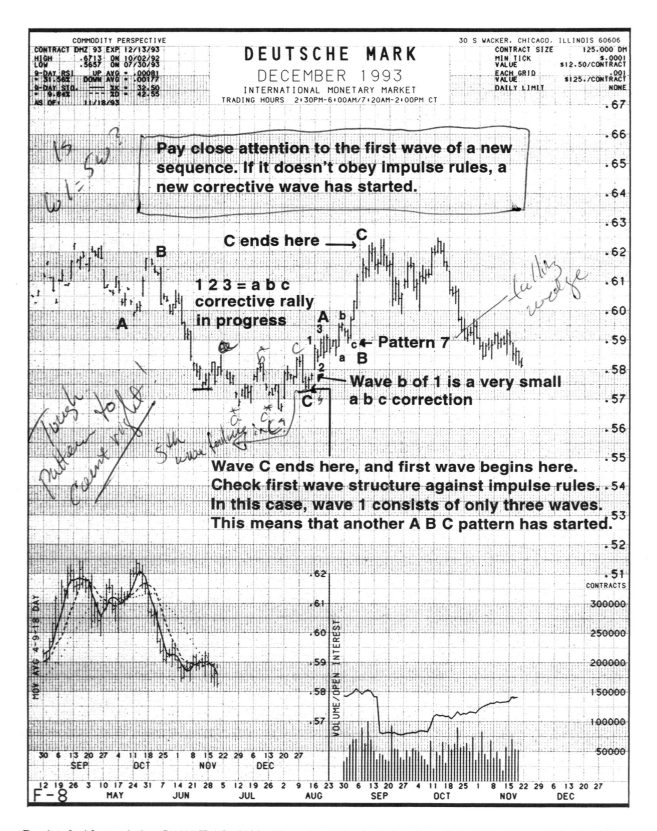

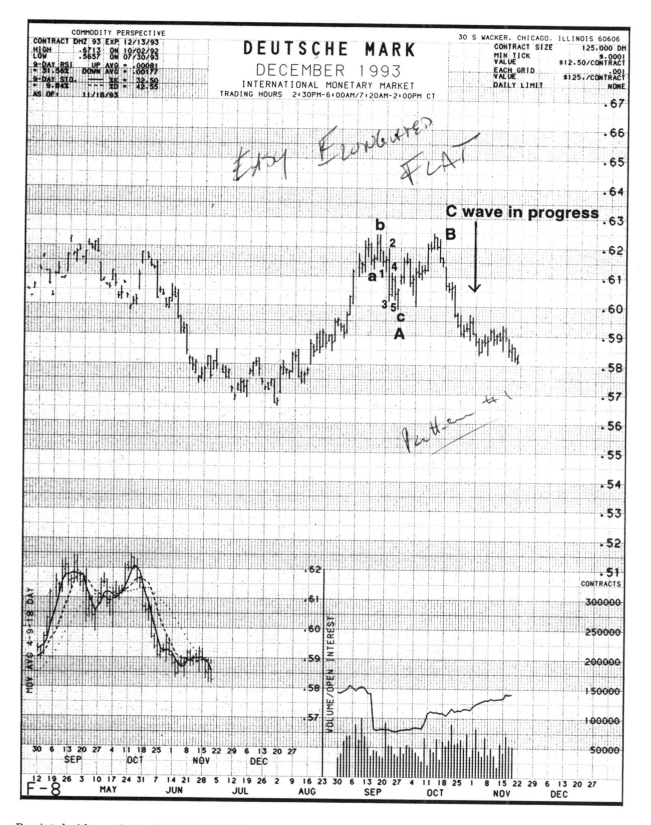

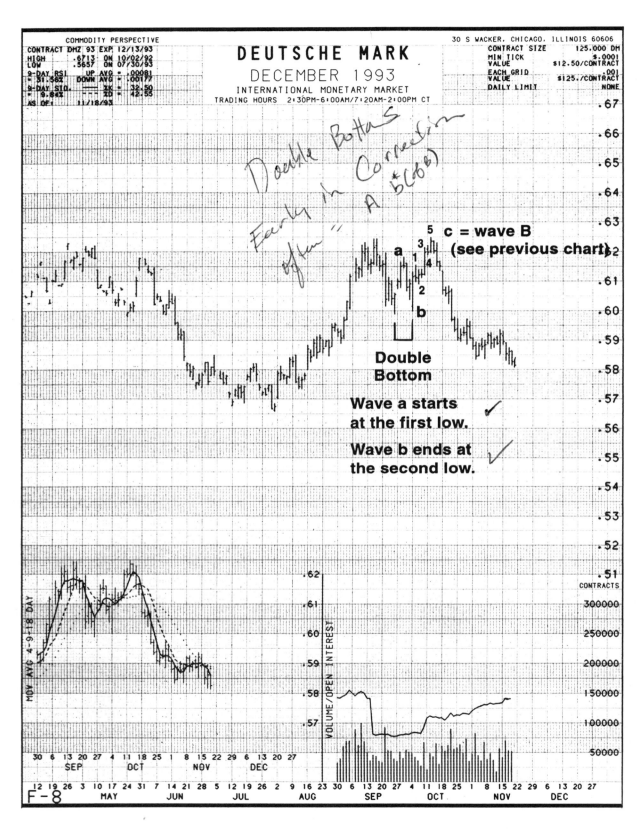

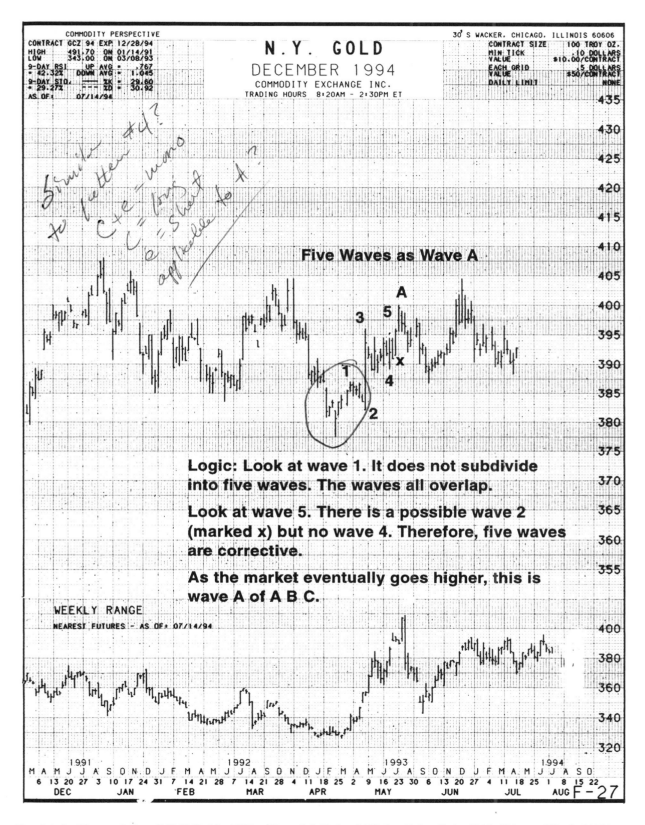

COMMODITY PERSPECTIVE

30' S WACKER, CHICAGO, ILLINOIS 60606

CONTRACT GCZ 94 EXP. 12/28/94
HIGH 491.70 ON 01/14/91
LOW 343.00 ON 03/08/93
9-DAY RSI UP AVG = .767
= 42.32% DOWN AVG = 1.045
9-DAY STO. %K = 29.60
= 29.27% %D = 30.92
AS OF: 07/14/94

CONTRACT SIZE 100 TROY OZ.
MIN TICK .10 DOLLARS
VALUE $10.00/CONTRACT
EACH GRID .5 DOLLARS
VALUE $50/CONTRACT
DAILY LIMIT NONE

N.Y. GOLD
DECEMBER 1994
COMMODITY EXCHANGE INC.
TRADING HOURS 8:20AM – 2:30PM ET

Five Waves as Wave A

Logic: Look at wave 1. It does not subdivide into five waves. The waves all overlap.

Look at wave 5. There is a possible wave 2 (marked x) but no wave 4. Therefore, five waves are corrective.

As the market eventually goes higher, this is wave A of A B C.

WEEKLY RANGE
NEAREST FUTURES - AS OF: 07/14/94

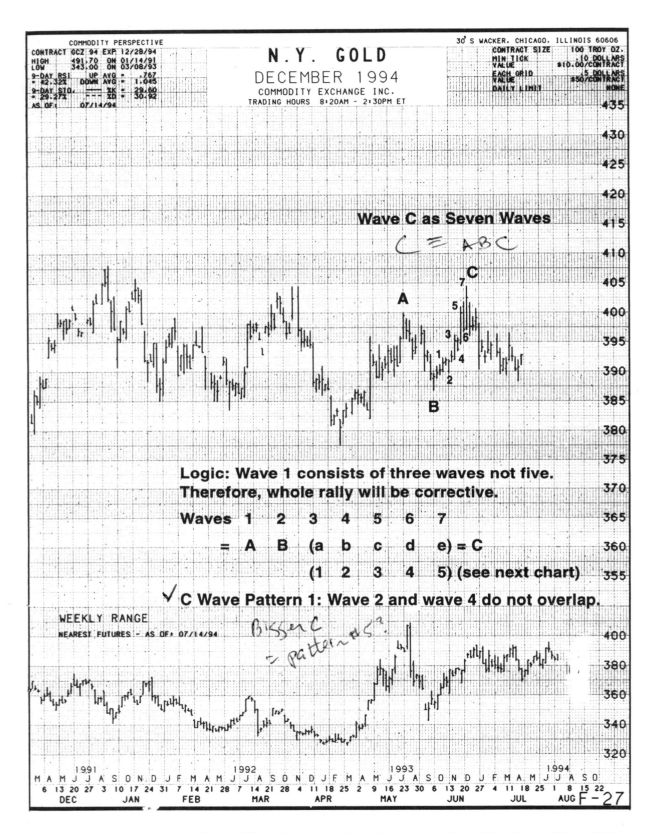

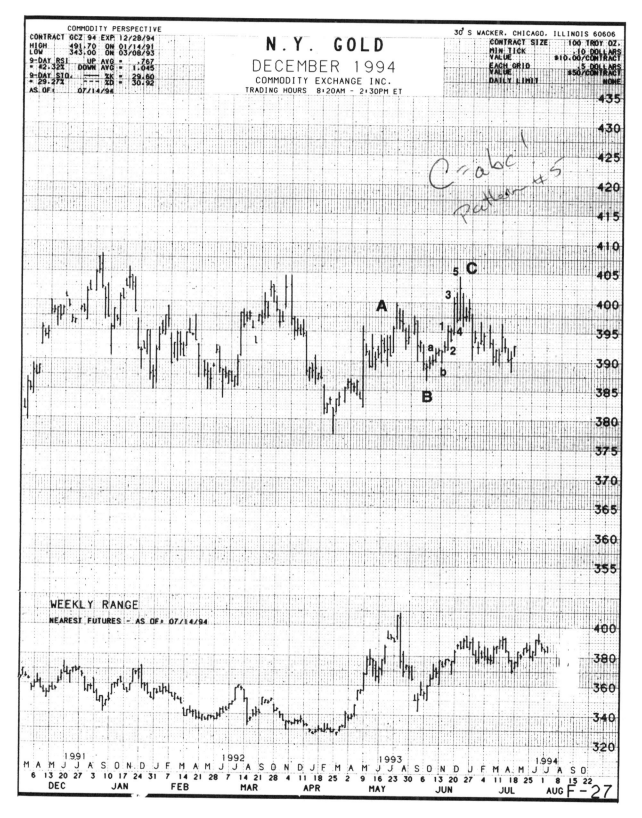

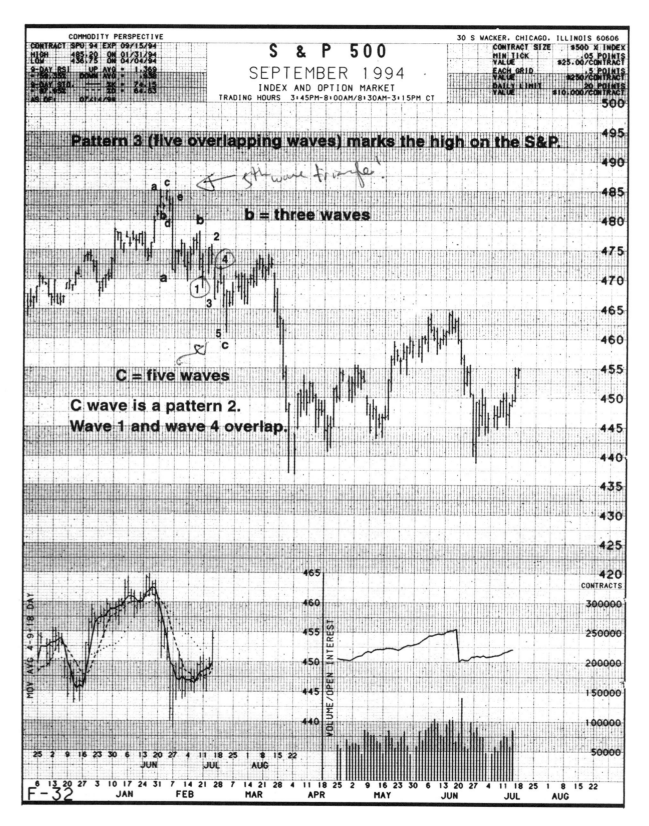

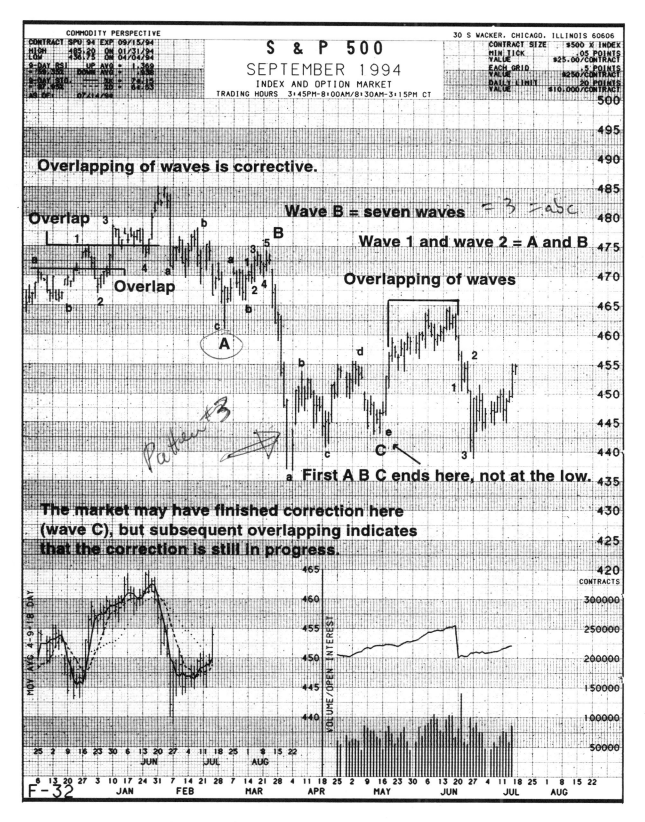

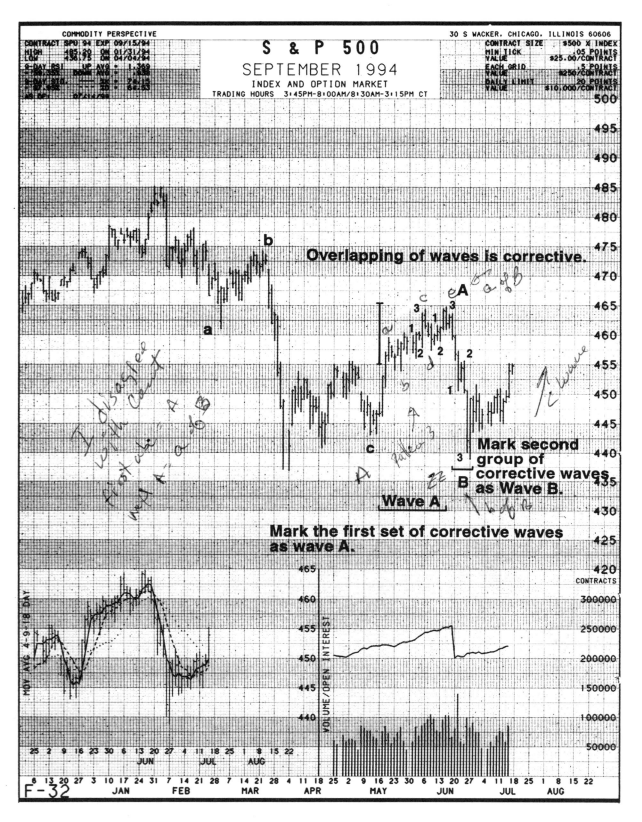

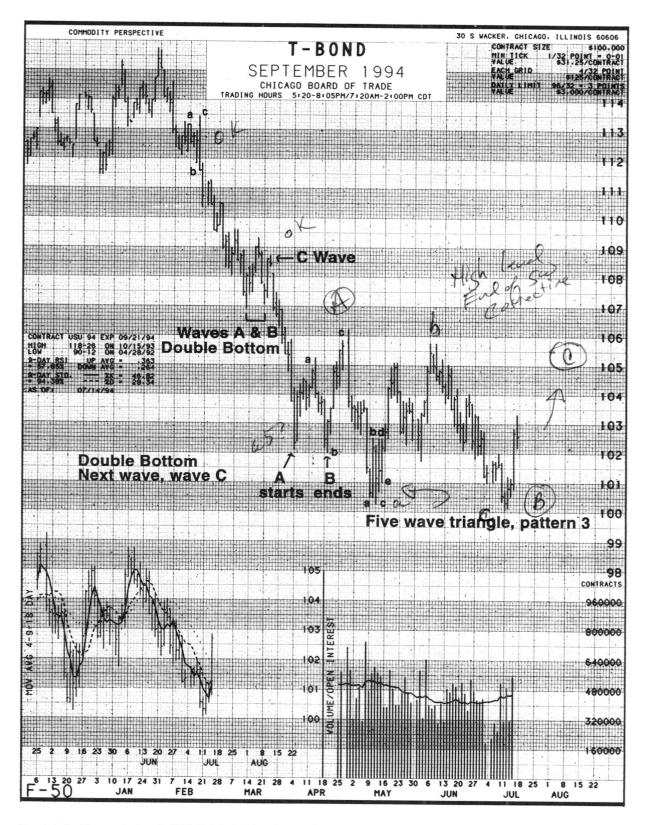

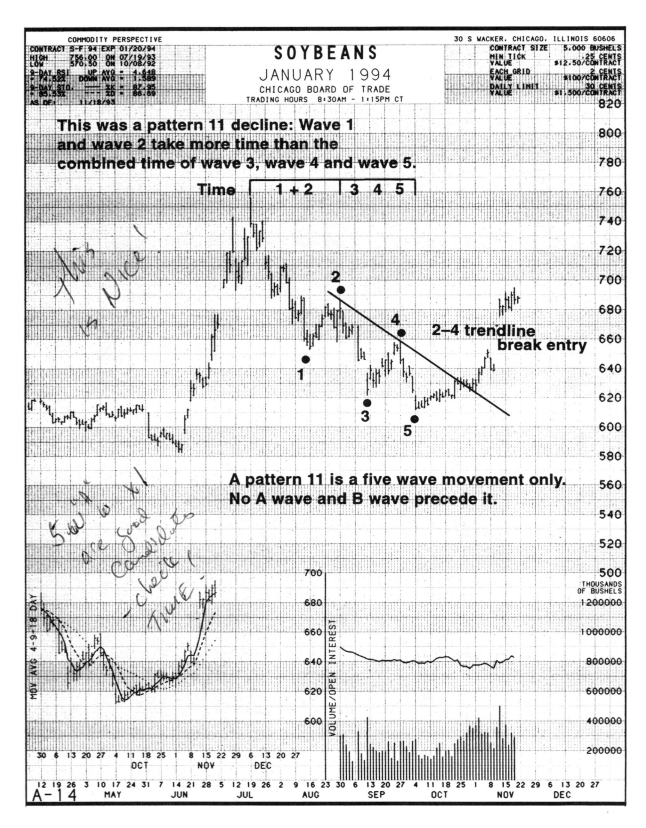

This was a pattern 11 decline: Wave 1 and wave 2 take more time than the combined time of wave 3, wave 4 and wave 5.

Time | 1 + 2 | 3 4 5

2–4 trendline break entry

A pattern 11 is a five wave movement only. No A wave and B wave precede it.

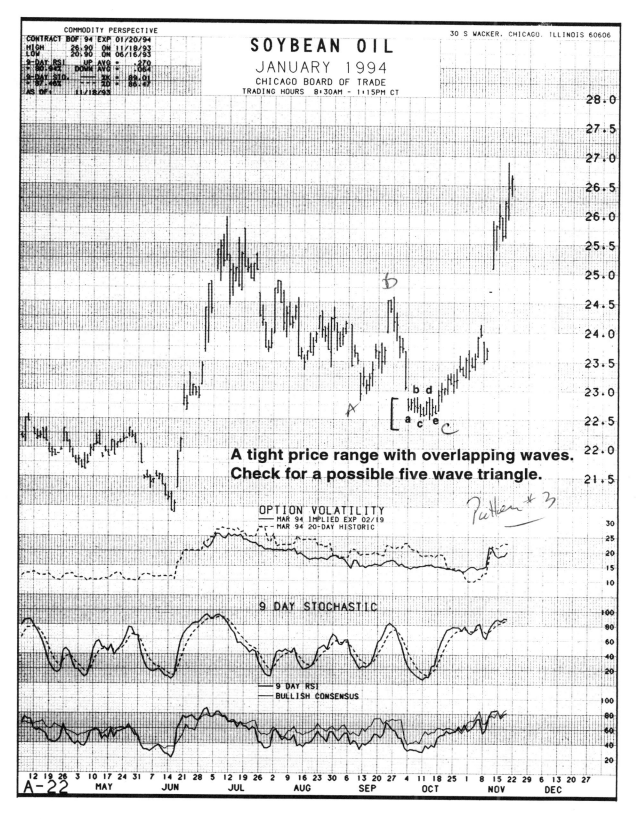

A tight price range with overlapping waves.
Check for a possible five wave triangle.

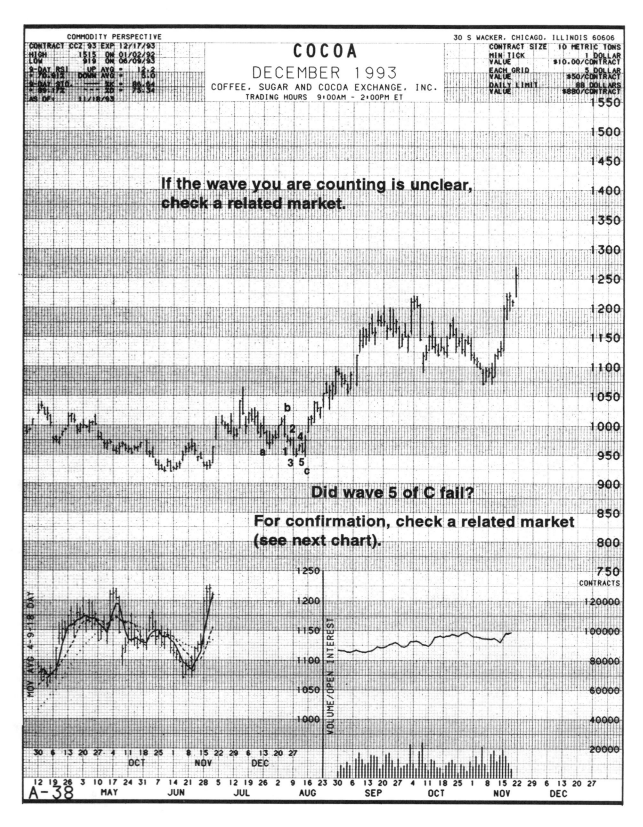

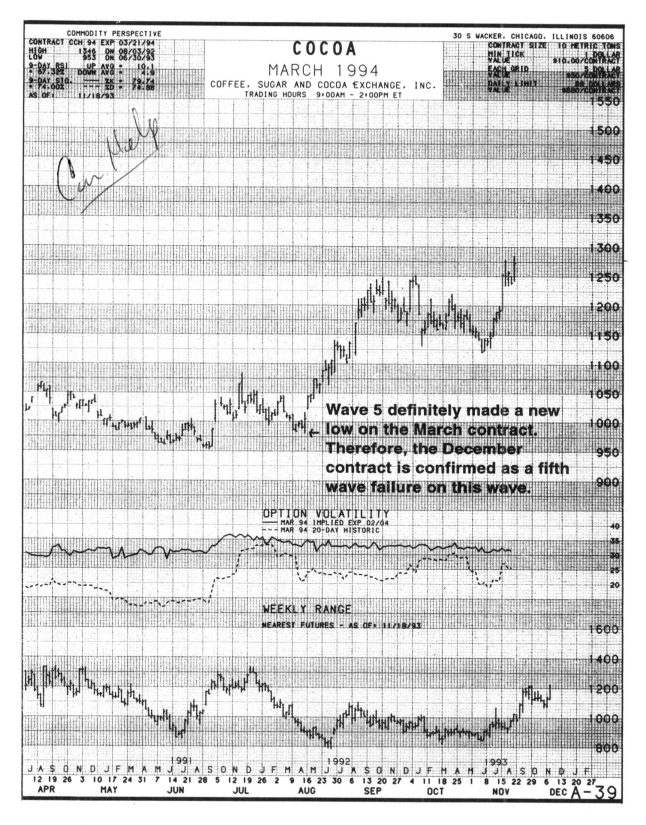

Wave 5 definitely made a new low on the March contract. Therefore, the December contract is confirmed as a fifth wave failure on this wave.

Chapter

5

C Wave Patterns

Using some of the basic Elliott Wave elements discussed in previous chapters, you can now apply them as a method of pattern recognition. The patterns, all some end form of A B C correction, are called *C wave patterns*.

Your goal is to stay out of the market until the pattern is just about to end. Your profit objective will always depend on whether the market is impulsive or corrective. If the market is impulsive, you will stay with the trade until the impulse wave that you have just joined is about to end. If the market is corrective, you will stay with the trade through the subsequent A B C. It is important to follow as many markets as you can because you only want to trade the most well-defined patterns. If the ideal pattern does not form, do not take the trade— save your capital for a better situation.

Note that all the following pattern rules deal with wave C only. It does not make a difference if the overall correction is a zigzag or a flat, or if the market is trending up or down.

[handwritten: SAME Patterns also present in A end of those as each of those can also end in a C wave.]

[handwritten: Also, same patterns exist at ALL DEGREES of TRENDS!]

[handwritten: STRATEGY]

[handwritten: So True!]

[handwritten: Also applicable elsewhere]

[handwritten: C of 2 and C of A and all of A / C of 4 and C* of B and all of B]*

81

The ideal trading strategy is to trade two contracts using the C wave patterns:

1. as a pattern recognition method to signal short-term trades with a fixed profit target, and

2. as a longer term trading approach pyramiding positions using further patterns as they develop and reversing positions only when a new trade is signaled by a new pattern.

Method Objective for Impulsive and Corrective Markets

The goal of the C wave method is to enter the market as soon as wave C completes.

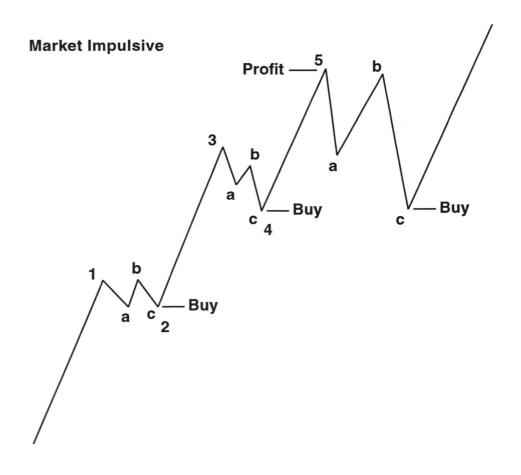

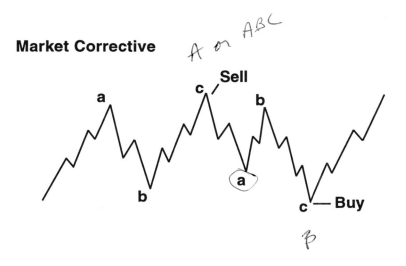

Market Corrective   A or ABC

Sell

a

c

b

b

a

c — Buy

B

Trade Strategy

Your goal is to identify pattern type and to find the end of wave C. If the overall market is *corrective*, look to find the end of wave C, then enter the market. Wait until completion of the next A B C before taking profits.

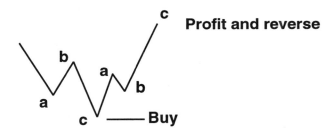

c **Profit and reverse**

b

a

a

b

c ——— **Buy**

If the market is *impulsive*, trend trade and use the end of correction 2 and correction 4 to add to your position. Wave 2 and wave 4 will end with some kind of C wave pattern.

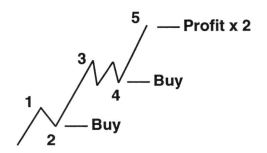

5 — **Profit x 2**

3

— **Buy**

1 4

2 — **Buy**

C Wave Patterns and Trading Rules

All C wave patterns consist of five waves with the exception of pattern 5. In all the C wave examples that follow, the use of small letters a, b, c, d, e are interchangeable with the use of the numbers 1, 2, 3, 4, 5. This holds true only for C waves.

Pattern 1

"Standard "FLAT" or "Zig-Zag"

A *pattern 1* can be recognized by the fact that wave 1 and wave 4 show no overlapping. Wave 2 and wave 4 may or may not show pattern alternation; they may be the same in time and in price or may look impulsive. A pattern 1 may follow all the rules of an impulse wave. However, what clearly defines the C wave pattern 1 from an impulse is that the larger wave A and wave B (of which wave C is the impulse) can be easily seen. The entry to a pattern 1 is a break of wave D. The stop then goes above/below the price high/low of wave E.

A & B = OBVIOUS

c ~ 5 waves

may or may not be impulsive

In the illustration below, pattern 1 looks impulsive; however, wave b and wave d

- will be the same in time and/or price,
- have simple price pullback, and
- show no pattern alternation.

(=a of C)

This could be a wave A of pattern 3. To prevent misinterpretation, do not enter the trade until the market breaks below/above wave d or subsequent price action shows that pattern 3 is not possible.

STD #1

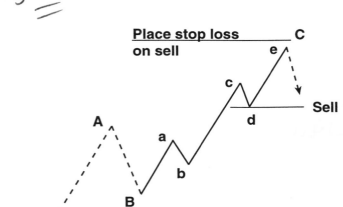

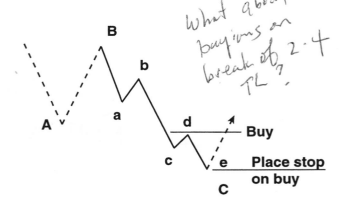

What about buying on break of 2-4 TL?

Same as 1 except
— C2 + C4 overlap (b+d) or touch
— C shorter

Pattern 2 "

A WEAK "C
with interval
overlapping
corrective
waves

In a C wave *pattern 2*, wave b and wave d overlap. Wave b and wave d may show pattern and time alternation. Wave e

- will be brief timewise, or may be a small five wave triangle,

- could, but might not, exceed the high/low of wave (c) of c.

The price move that follows will probably be quite slow. However, this will be the end of wave C, so a certain amount of patience is needed.

STD #2

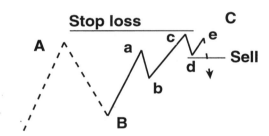

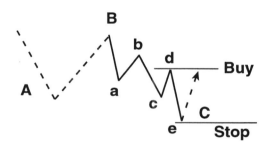

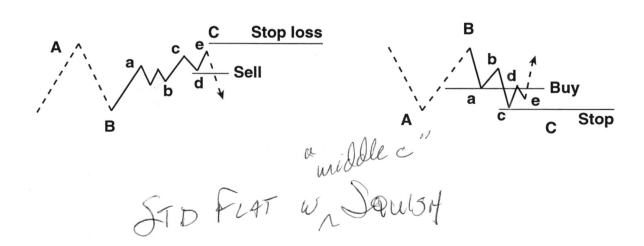

"middle c"

STD FLAT w, SQUISH

C – "STALL" ("a" long) & endig triangle

Pattern 3

C TRIANGLES with long wave -a!

"a" Big 7 B!

A *pattern 3*, which is a five wave triangle, is a highly reliable end pattern and occurs frequently. <u>Wave a is by far the longest price wave.</u> Wave a may consist of three waves or five waves.

Wave b, wave c, wave d and wave e

- will have similar price range,
- will possibly skew, and
- will show similar subdivisions.

Wave e will be very brief timewise unless wave e is in itself a smaller five wave triangle. The entry to a pattern 3 is a break of wave d.

Strong "a" Triangles

"A wave PROBE

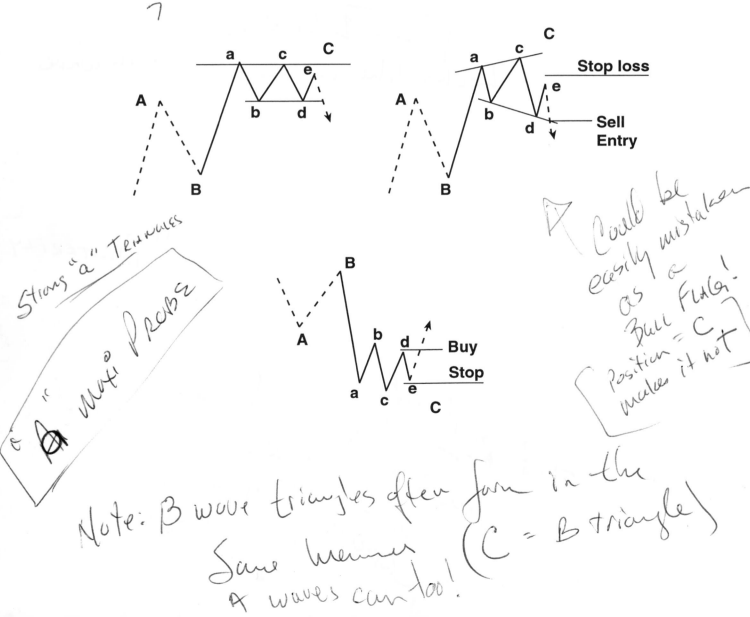

Could be easily mistaken as a Bull Flag! Position = C makes it not

Note: B wave triangles often form in the same manner (C = B triangle) A waves can too!

"C STALL"

("c" longer t/o ending triangle) / 3 - 3 - 1 - 3 - 1

" C corrective "

Pattern 4

C = abcde
- non-impulsive !
- non-triangle !

In a *pattern 4*, wave C consists of five clear waves. Waves a and b will both subdivide into three smaller waves. Wave C will be one wave. Wave d will subdivide into three smaller waves. Wave e will be one wave.

little "c" = long + mono !
little "e" = short + mono !

W Flag (Bear & fly)
(following   3-3 following AB)

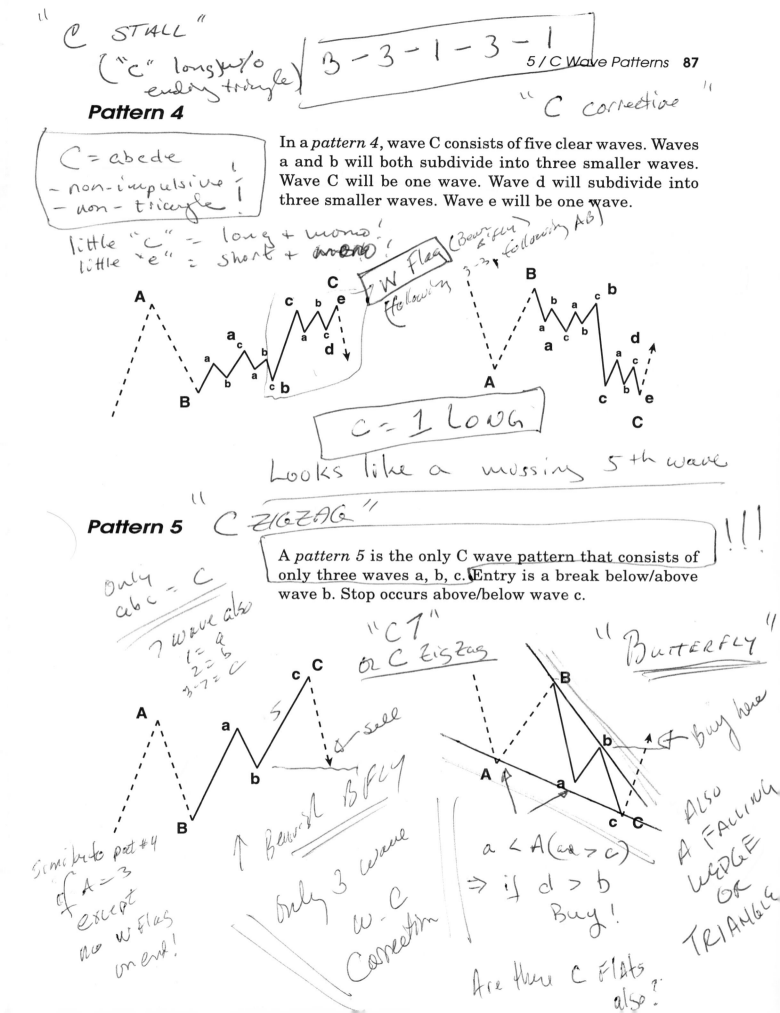

C = 1 LONG

Looks like a missing 5th wave

Pattern 5   " C ZIGZAG "

A *pattern 5* is the only C wave pattern that consists of only three waves a, b, c. Entry is a break below/above wave b. Stop occurs above/below wave c.   !!!

only abc = C

7 wave also
1 = a
2 = b
3-7 = c

"C7"
or C Zigzag

" BUTTERFLY "

↓ sell

↗ buy here

Bearish BFLY

Only 3 wave
w. C
Correction

a < A (a a > c)
⇒ if d > b
Buy !

ALSO
A FALLING
WEDGE
OR
TRIANGLE

Similar to part #4
of A = 3 except
no W flags
on end!

Are there C Flats
also ?

Strong B Waves and Trading Rules

Pattern 6, an A B C running correction, is a very common correction. At first glance, it is hard to see the A B C pattern because of the length of wave B. Wave C is always a triangle, wave C can pull back into the price area of wave A, but most of the trading will be done above/below this. Traditionally, this pattern is known as a *double three*, and the B wave is labeled as X.

This long B wave concept can be used as a springboard to the other patterns that until now have not been classified. When a running correction is found in a trending market, the move after wave C completes is always strong. This does not hold true in a corrective market where this pattern often gives a false appearance of price strength. If you are trading in a market that appears to be strong but does not obey all the impulse market rules, check for the A B C running correction or its variation patterns 7, 8 and 9. Entry for patterns 6, 7, 8 and 9 is a break of wave d.

Patterns 6, 7, 8 and 9 all have strong B waves that end well above the beginning of wave A.

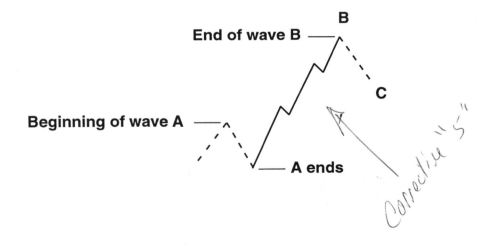

ALL DOUBLE 3s = RUNNING! (see pattern #3)

End of wave B ——— **B**

C

Beginning of wave A ———

A ends

Corrective "5"

The more likely B wave is one brisk movement with no subdivisions or an obvious three wave a b c.

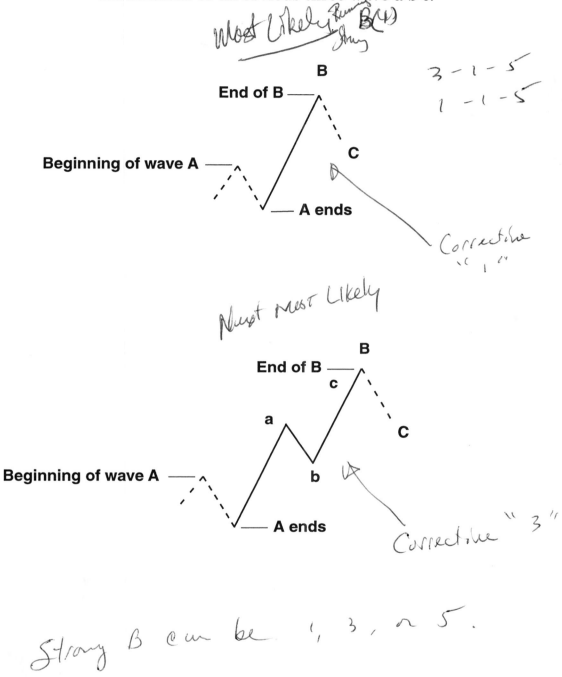

Most Likely Running B(4)
Strong

3 - 1 - 5
1 - 1 - 5

B

End of B

C

Beginning of wave A

A ends

Corrective "C₁"

Next Most Likely

B

End of B

c

a

C

Beginning of wave A

b

A ends

Corrective "3"

Strong B can be 1, 3, or 5.

STRONG "B" = Running TRIANGLE (normal a, e)

Pattern 6

A strong B wave, *pattern 6* is an A B C running correction.

C = TRIANGLE (ALWAYS) (3)
B = Strong (3)
A = "

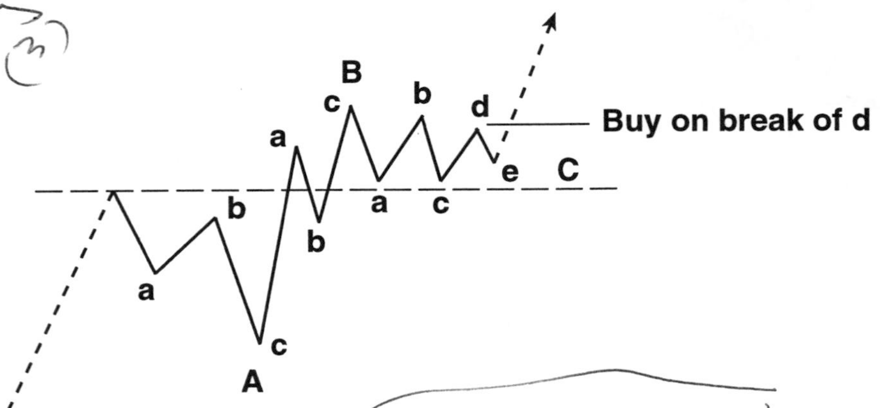

B
c
b
d
Buy on break of d
a
e
C
b
a
c
b
a
c
A

Big B w C Δ

"Money"

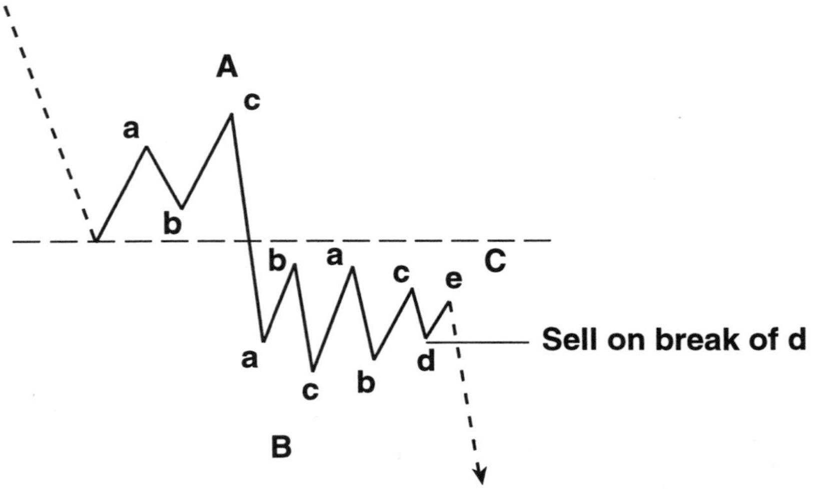

A
c
a
b
b
a
c
e
C
Sell on break of d
a
d
c
b
B

Note: SAME AS PATTERN #3
Except here it follows an A wave
and a of C = B
this adds one wave to triangle
since old "a" of C = B.

Pattern 7

In a *pattern 7*, a strong B wave, wave C consists of five waves and must retrace at least 50 percent (or more) of wave B. Wave C could pull back into the price area of wave A but does not have to if wave B is very long.

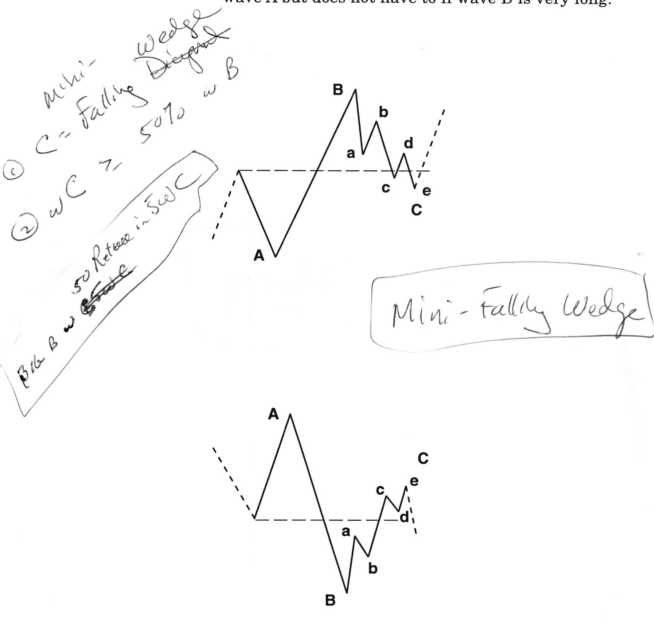

Mini- Falling Wedge
① C = Falling Diagonal Wedge
② wC ≥ 50% w B

50 Retrace in 5wC
Big B w

STRONG "B" = Running Triangle (large a)

" a Running Wedge (large a)

Pattern 8 "Running Pattern #3"

In a *pattern 8*, a strong B wave, wave C may or may not come back into the price range of wave A. Wave C must be a pattern 3 (five overlapping waves). Wave a (of C) is the largest in the final a b c d e pattern.

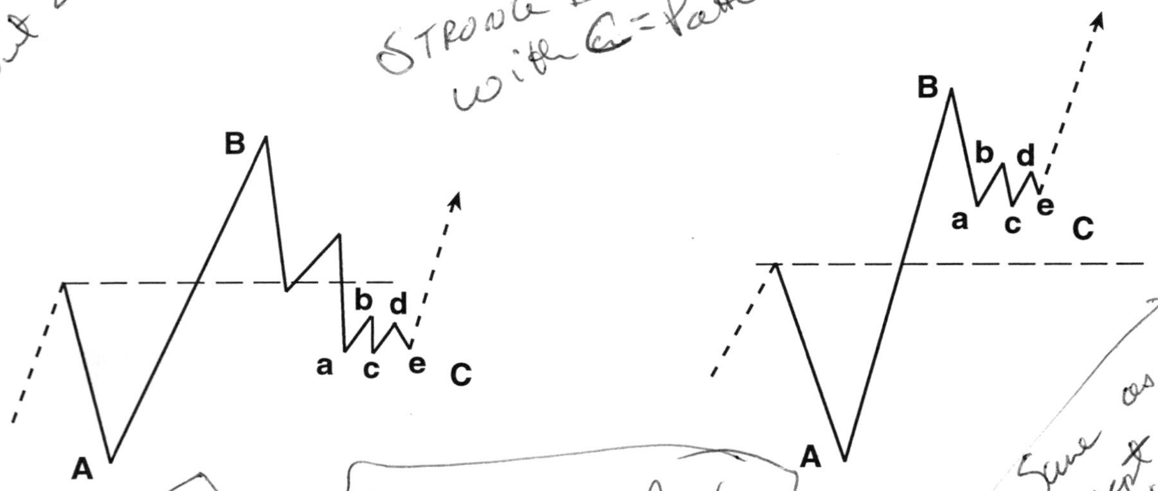

Big "a" but < B!

STRONG B with C = Pattern #3

C ▵ w "a" PROBE

"a" mini Probe

Same as C ▵ except C has (large a) rel. relative to bcde.

Wave a is the largest in this final a b c d e pattern.

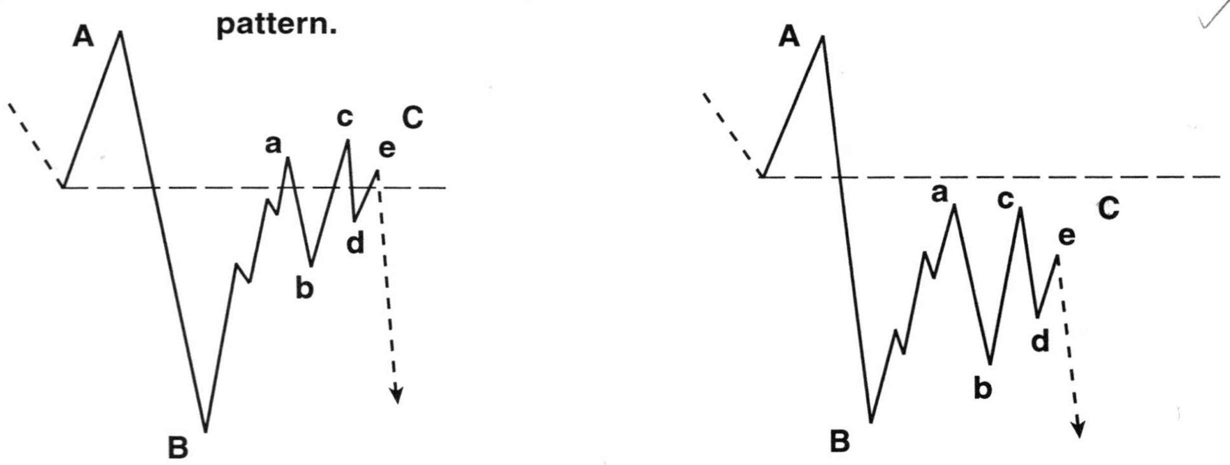

Same as "C STALL" = long "a" w ending triangle (pattern #3) except it has strong B.

C TRIANGLE STRONG "B" = Running TRIANGLE
with Big "e" ~ wA (Long e)

Pattern 9

Pattern #3
except
"e" of C D = long
(instead of "a")

In a *pattern 9*, wave B may be of any type (zigzag, flat or strong B wave). Wave C is an a b c d in an overlapping price area with wave e making a strong but temporary break in the direction of the first (largest) wave A. The entry point is a break of wave d with a stop loss 50 percent of wave e.

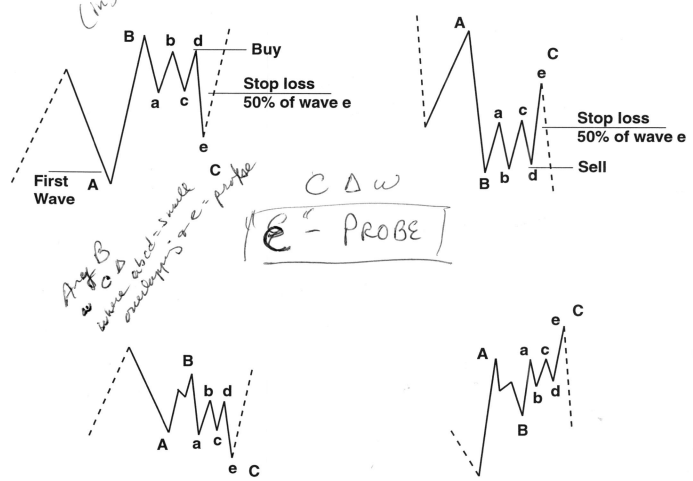

Any B
& C D = small
where abcd = small
overlapping + e-probe

C Δ W

"e" - PROBE

C stall with ends triangle or long "e"

Five Wave Corrections and Trading Rules

Handwritten left margin notes:

2   STD   — normal c of C
           — short c of C

2   C Stall ~~ending triangles~~
    long a   w ending △
    __ long C w/o ending △

↑   Butterfly (3 wave C!)

4   Strong "B" followed by C with
           ending △s

Pattern 10

Handwritten:
• Normal C △ (are)
• Normal C wedge (are)
• long a
    into C △
    into C wedge
• long c @ end of
    C △
    c wedge

2 Falsie "5's"

• x ZZ w ending △
, x w1 w "w2" = Flat
        "w4" = triangle
    ↳ Violates Time Rule
Rule: Time of w3 + w4 + w5
        > time of w1 + w2
in this case, it is not!

Two more corrective patterns that I have discovered are not strictly C waves but are corrective nonetheless. I think of these patterns as fitting into the same category as B wave triangles inasmuch as the market action after they finish can be predicted. These two patterns—10 and 11—are complete corrections in themselves, and the price move that follows will retrace most if not all the pattern.

Pattern 10 is a zigzag pattern (wave B retraces 61.8 percent or less of wave A). However, note that not all zigzags are a pattern 10.

Handwritten right: 3 wave patterns that ≡ ABC! aka False 5's

Unfortunately, wave C gives a false pattern signal and then goes on to make a new high.

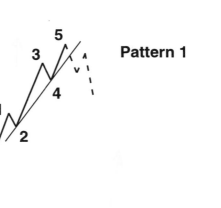

Pattern 1

Handwritten right: Normal zig-zag

MOCK Impulse
= ZS + Zag + triangle

A new high must end in a five wave triangle.

not really impulsive

Another 3 wave C ?!
Zig-Zag "extended"
with ending triangle

Entry: A break of wave d

always simple abc
always < AB (w2)
in price + time!

False Signal
that a
Pattern 1
STD ZZ completed
(keep to Recognition)
(1) "w4" = simple ABC < the price of "w2"
(2) (a) > a
(3) ending triangle

Pattern 10 can easily be mistaken for an impulse, but the wave 4 (in the first diagram) will always be smaller in price and time than wave 2. Also wave 4 will be a simple A B C, never anything more complex. Entry is a break of wave D.

"FALSIE #1"

Incorrect Count

Simple a b c

Wave 4 is smaller in both price and time when compared to wave 2.

Correct Count

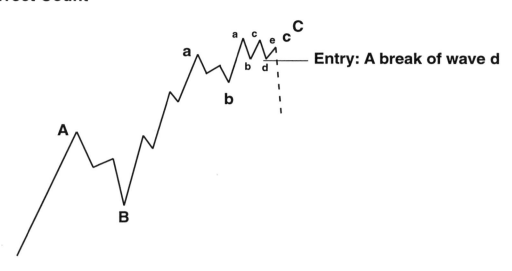

Pattern 11

A false impulse similar to pattern 10, *pattern 11* could at first be mistaken as an impulse. The deciding factor is that the combined time of wave 3, wave 4 and wave 5 (when measured from the end of wave 2) is equal to less than wave 1 or wave 2 combined. Some of the subwaves on close inspection may be 3s not (impulsive) 5s. A pattern 11 could be completely retraced or may be wave A of a larger A B C. Entry is a break of 2 – 4 trendline stop above/below wave 5.

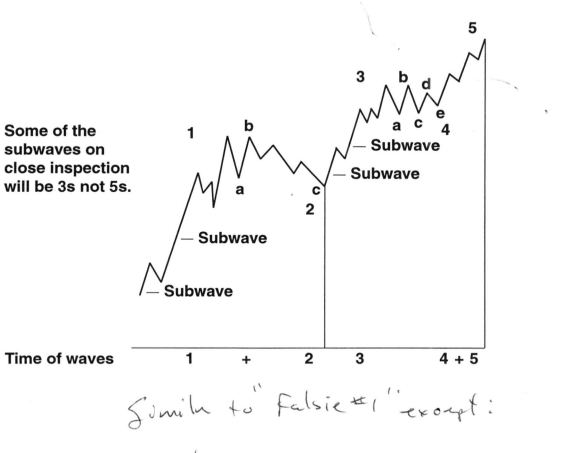

Some of the subwaves on close inspection will be 3s not 5s.

1 b a c 2

— Subwave

— Subwave

3 b d a c e 4 5

— Subwave

— Subwave

Time of waves   1   +   2   3   4 + 5

Similar to "Falsie #1" except:

① No $w5$ $\triangle$

② Some subwaves — 3 (possibly)

* ③ Time of $(w1 + w2) \geq (w3 + w4 + w5)$

If $3 + 4 + 5 < 1 + 2$

$\Rightarrow$ NOT IMPULSE!

List of C Wave Patterns

For easy reference, a complete visual list of the C wave patterns follows.

Pattern 1   No overlapping of wave 1 and wave 4

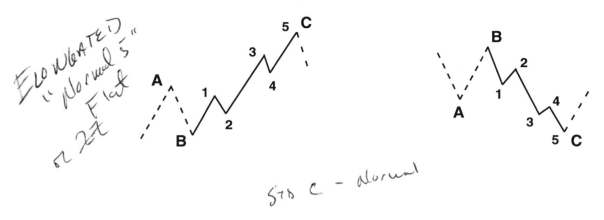

Pattern 2   Wave b and wave d overlap

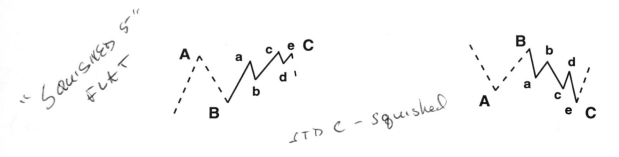

Pattern 2

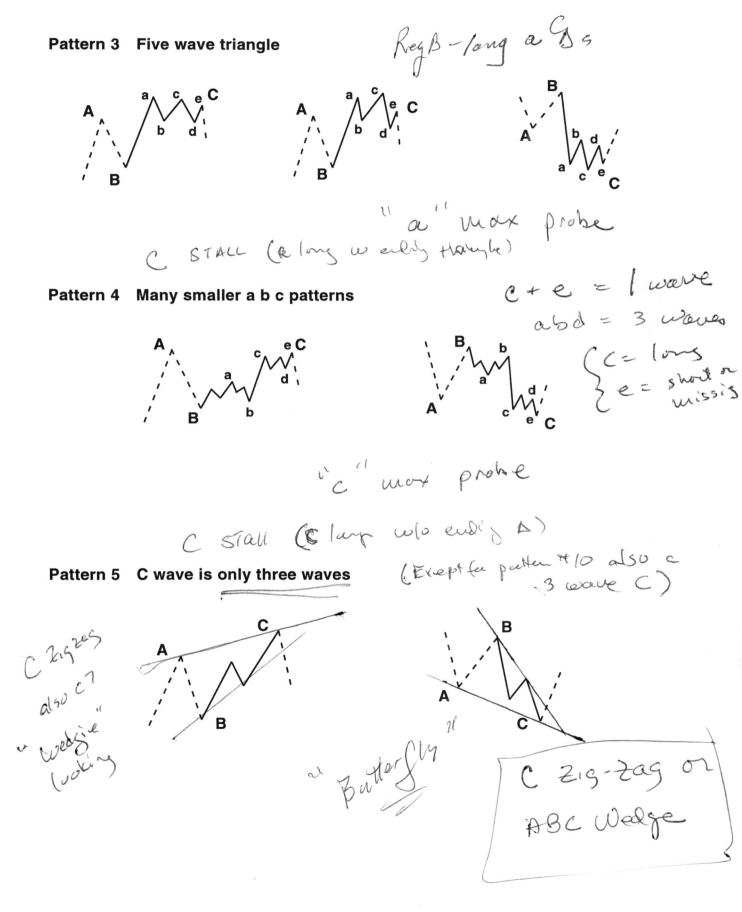

Pattern 3   Five wave triangle

RegB - long a C's

"a" max probe

C STALL (& long w ending triangle)

Pattern 4   Many smaller a b c patterns

c + e = 1 wave

a b d = 3 waves

{ c = long
{ e = short or missing

"c" max probe

C STALL (C long w/o ending △)

(Except for pattern #10 also c 3 wave C)

Pattern 5   C wave is only three waves

C Zigzags

also c7

" wedgie" looking

" Butterfly"

C Zig-zag or ABC Wedge

Pattern 6 Strong B wave ending in five waves

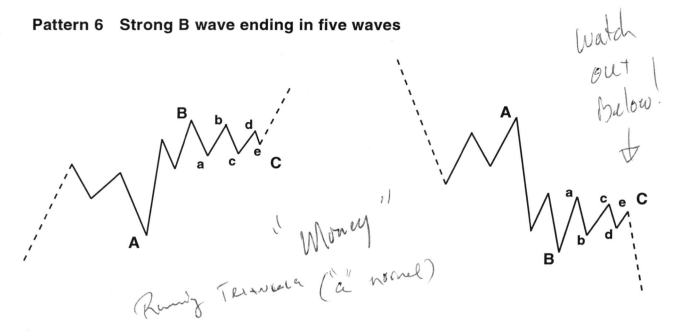

"Money"

Running Triangle ("a" normal)

watch out Below!

Pattern 7 Strong B wave that is retraced 50 percent or more by wave C

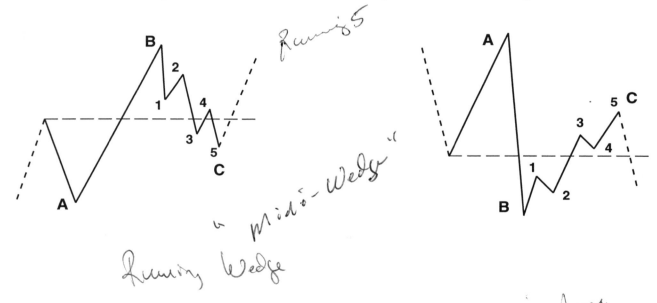

Running 5

"Midi-Wedge"

Running Wedge

a long
~ Zig-Zag 5 crunch

Pattern 8 Strong B wave ending in a five wave triangle

"Money" with "a" more

Running Big a 1 ®

long B
long a
Big B a

Pattern 8

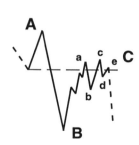 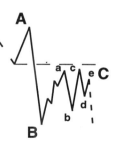

Pattern 9 **Wave a, wave b, wave c and wave d overlap, but wave e makes a strong break in the direction of wave A**

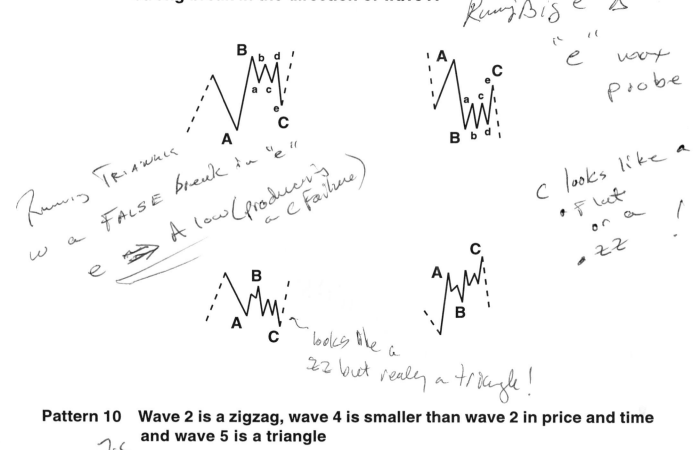

Runny Big e A

" "

"e" wont probe

Runny TRIANGLE w a FALSE break in "e"

e ➜ A low (producing a c failure)

c looks like a Flat or a ZZ!

looks like a ZZ but really a triangle!

Pattern 10 **Wave 2 is a zigzag, wave 4 is smaller than wave 2 in price and time and wave 5 is a triangle**

Super ZigZags = ZZ + △

FALSE #1

= ABC or A

Pattern 11 **Total time of wave 1 and wave 2 is greater than or equal to the combined times of wave 3, wave 4 and wave 5**

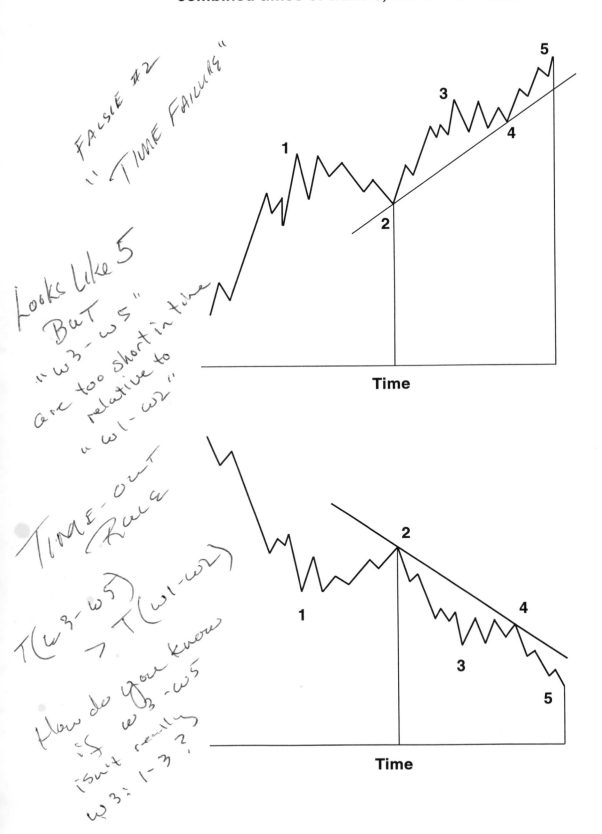

Time

Time

Handwritten annotations:

FALSIE #2
" TIME FAILURE"

Looks Like 5
BuT
" W3 - W5 "
are too short in time
relative to
" W1 - W2 "

TIME - OUT
Rule

T(W3 - W5)
> T(W1 - W2)

How do you know
if W3 - W5
isn't really
W3: 1 - 3 ?

How To Find
C Wave Patterns

C wave patterns are found at the end of areas of price congestion on intraday and daily charts. Check these areas for waves A and B, then start matching against the rules for C wave patterns described in Chapter 5.

Or when the market has been moving strongly up or down, look for the first price pullback and mark as a possible wave A. If the next wave in the direction of the trend is corrective (three waves or five waves showing no impulse rules), mark as wave B. Now check the daily wave flows (see Chapter 3), and check for a match against the C wave pattern rules. Place entry stops in the market as indicated by the pattern rules.

To help your search for C wave patterns, try the following techniques:

- Use a transparent overlay to trace possible wave flows without marking your charts.

- Make a larger copy of the daily chart to make it easier to see every wave.

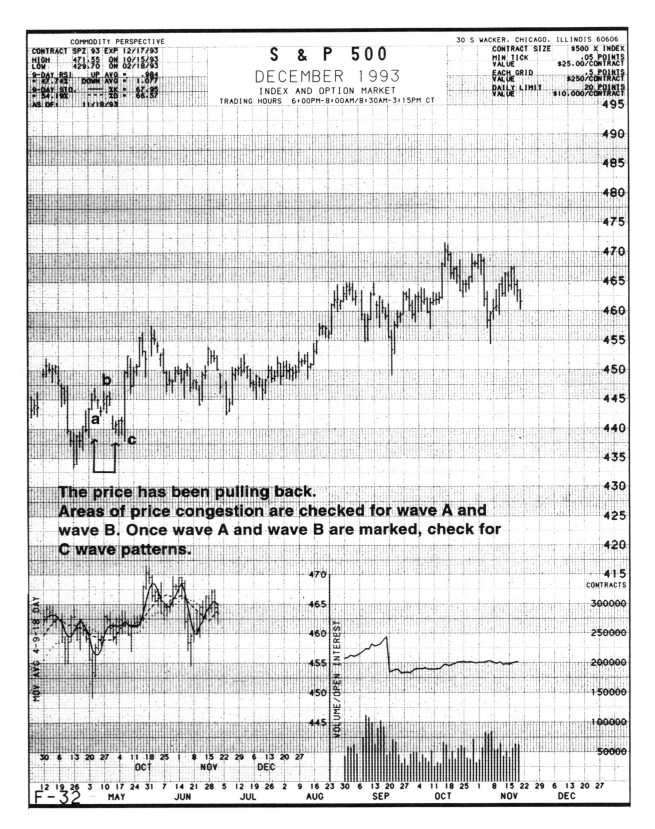

The price has been pulling back. Areas of price congestion are checked for wave A and wave B. Once wave A and wave B are marked, check for C wave patterns.

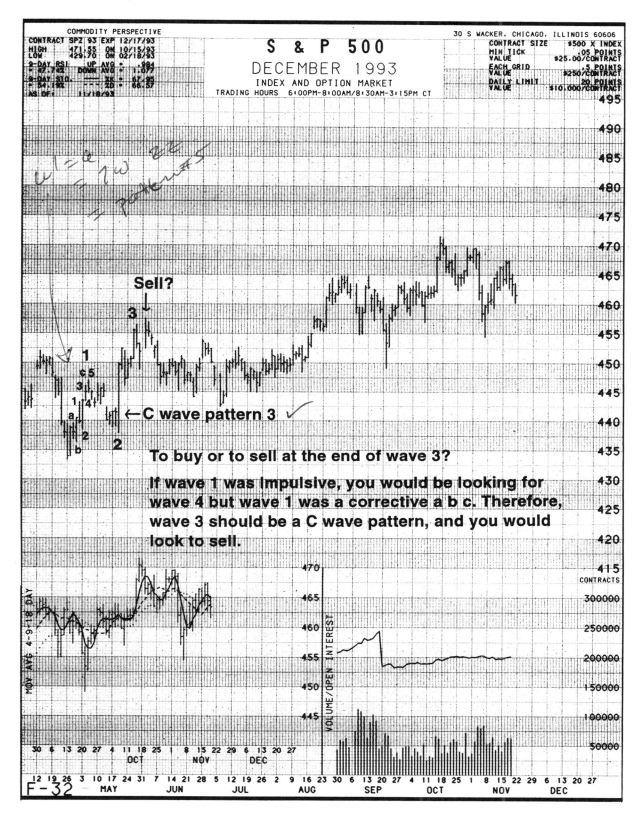

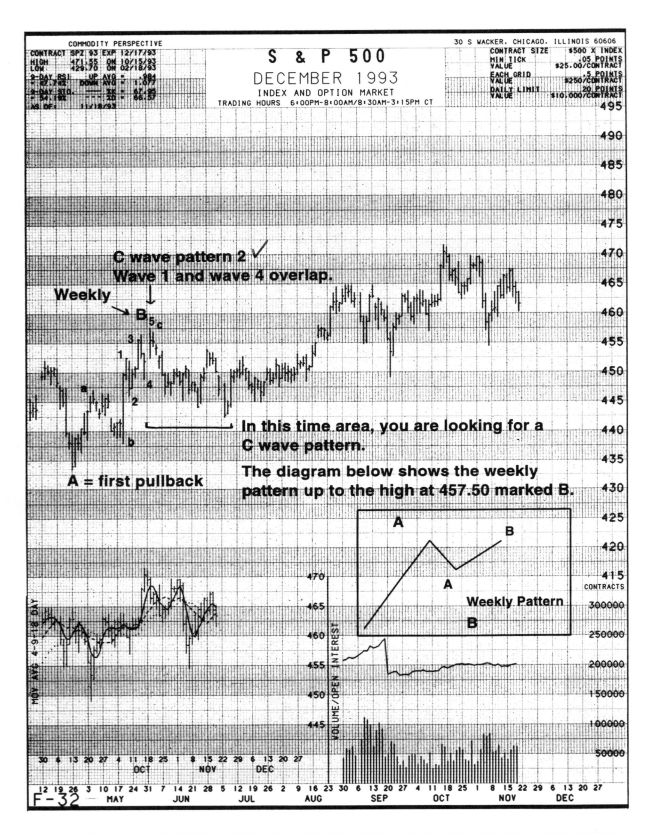

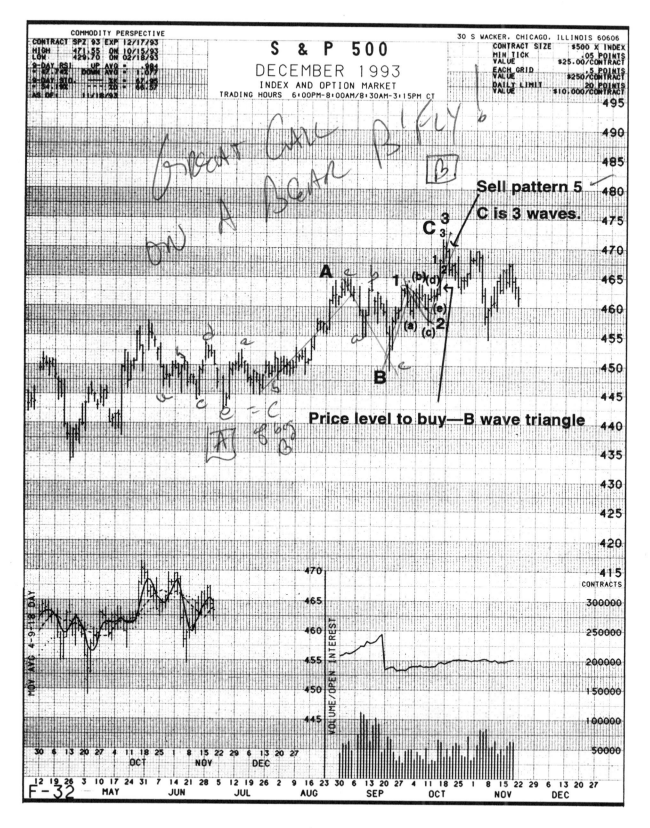

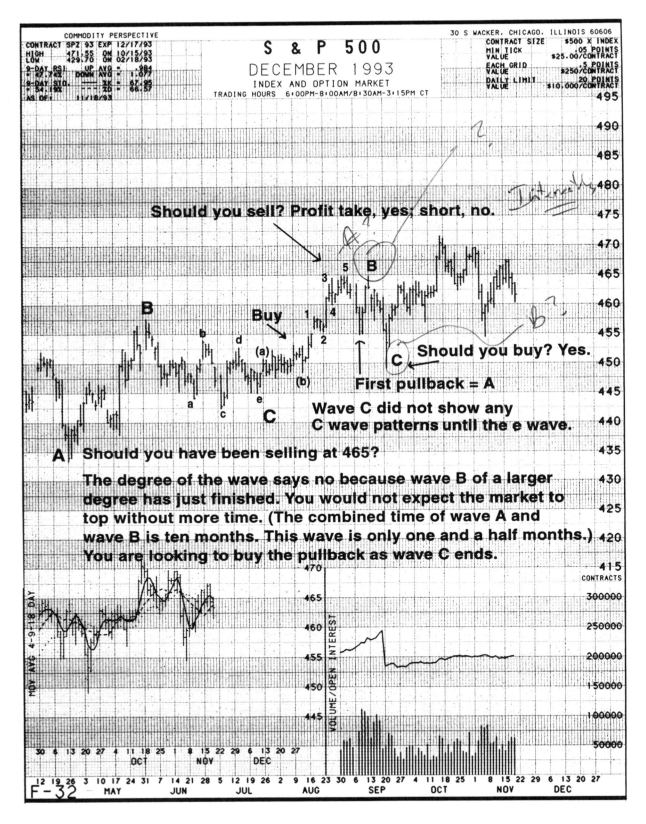

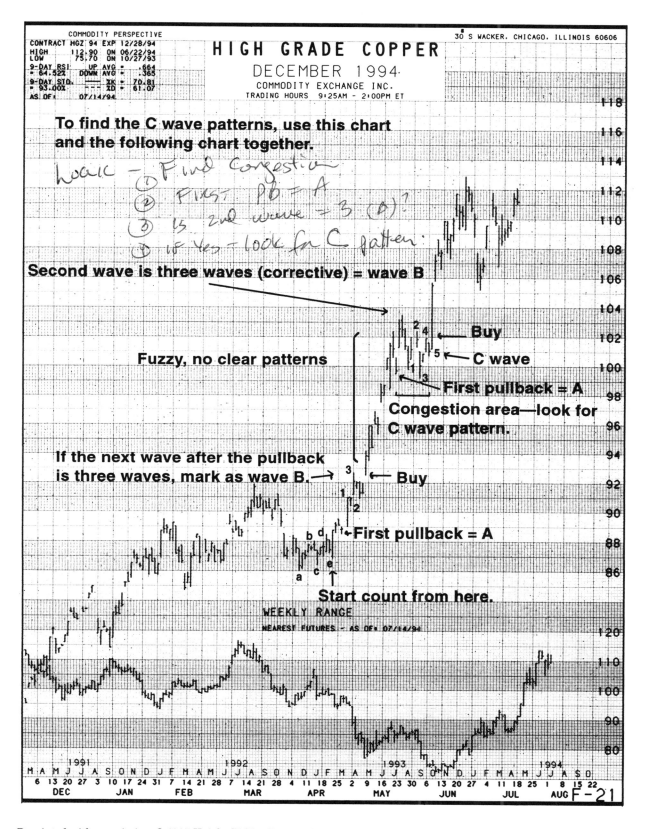

To find the C wave patterns, use this chart and the following chart together.

Logic — ① Find Congestion
② First PB = A
③ Is 2nd wave = 3 (B)?
④ If yes — look for C pattern.

Second wave is three waves (corrective) = wave B

Fuzzy, no clear patterns

Buy
C wave
First pullback = A
Congestion area—look for C wave pattern.

If the next wave after the pullback is three waves, mark as wave B. →

Buy

First pullback = A

Start count from here.

WEEKLY RANGE
NEAREST FUTURES - AS OF: 07/14/94

HIGH GRADE COPPER
DECEMBER 1994
COMMODITY EXCHANGE INC.
TRADING HOURS 9:25AM - 2:00PM ET

COMMODITY PERSPECTIVE
30 S WACKER, CHICAGO, ILLINOIS 60606

CONTRACT HGZ 94 EXP 12/28/94
HIGH 112.90 ON 06/22/94
LOW 75.70 ON 10/27/93
9-DAY RSI UP AVG .664
= 64.52% DOWN AVG .365
9-DAY STO. XK 70.81
= 93.00% XD 61.07
AS OF: 07/14/94

F-21

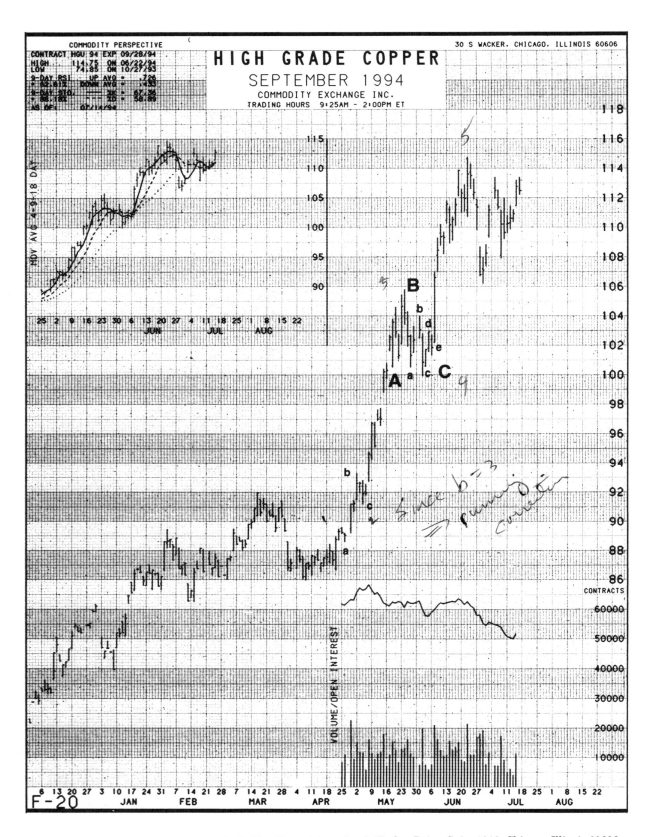

Chapter

7

Profit Takes

One of the most difficult concepts of trading is *profit takes*. I am a strong believer in trying to make something out of every trade because in the past a lot of money has slipped away through trying to trend trade what in hindsight turned out to be a choppy market.

With the guidance of Elliott's wave principles, you will find it easier to read the market. Often you will be able to predict what is going to happen before the crowd does. This means that you will be early, often by months. Predicting time is extremely difficult. The problem is: You can see where the next major move is headed, so you hold onto every C wave pattern for the big trend trade only to find that on a larger degree every wave series will stretch timewise to the very end. The net result is: You have made a lot of profitable trades that have turned to break-even or even losses after you consider the impact of brokerage and have wasted several months of your time.

"2 chunks"
positions

1 The solution is to trade some contracts for quick profits while continuing to hold others for the trend trade. Trend trading is dependent on wave degree, exit and reverse only when the big patterns emerge. After a true trend has begun, you can add more long-term positions using the C wave patterns.

2 I use margin requirements as a profit take measure. The exchange margin is usually lower than your brokerage house requires, but I like to use the higher figure since it is a true measure of return. Margin increases with volatility and thus to some extent remains in step with the market. When ranges are tight, margins are small and a fixed profit based on margin is going to give a realistic return.

Illustrated on the chart that follows, the profit takes are all based on a percentage of margin that varies from market to market. The percentage return on the S&P is only 50 percent because the margin is always fairly high when compared to the average price range. On the currencies, I use 100 percent return. Intraday profit takes must naturally be smaller because the wave degree that you are trading is only minor.

This chart demonstrates why fixed profit takes can be preferable to trend trading. There are many clear patterns, but stop and reverse strategies are too slow because of the limited range.

Alternate Counts and Recounts

" Discovering C Wave Patterns "

Good Title

In the markets, your analysis will often be wrong—this is simply a fact of life. However, unless you have too rigid a view of where the market is going, this should not hinder your ability to make money. With the C wave patterns, you must be prepared to trade the patterns as you find them.

A good strategy, if possible, is to always trade two contracts, even if that means trading minicontracts. You can take quick profits on one position and let the other one ride until you find another clear pattern. Now that you have discovered C wave patterns, you will see them in all markets. C wave patterns occur frequently on intraday charts. You can wait and conserve your capital for the best trades.

Instead of looking at only one or two markets, investigate a variety of markets. *Alternate counts* are necessary because the Elliott Wave is flexible by nature and when a perfect pattern sets up, then fails and changes into something else, it is because fundamental information has entered the market. Alternate counts will not change the nature of the move—if you are in an impulsive market, the market will remain impulsive. And if you are in a corrective market, unless it is the very end of the correction, you still stay in a corrective market.

These factors make it difficult for long-term counting. This is why you will find Elliott Wave analysts saying different things. Until a final wave is over, there is always the possibility of an extension (for instance, wave C corrections sometimes can go on for many months, even years). In the currencies and the grains, large price moves have been made during the last five or six years, but all the moves were of a corrective nature rather than impulsive. These corrective waves last a very long time, and there are a lot of small C wave patterns within the longer corrections. This allows you ample opportunity to make a profit; you do not need a long-term view. (See the December Deutschemark Charts in Chapter 4).

Recounts are required when waves subdivide. The objective is to get the best possible count. Alternate counts will often yield the same buy/sell signals, in which case final labeling choice is a matter of personal preference as long as all the pattern and wave count rules are satisfied.

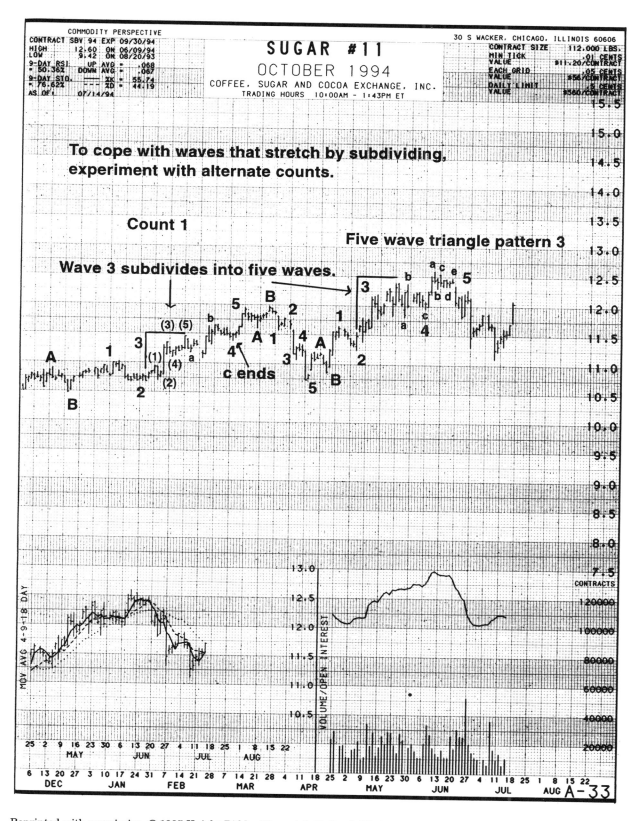

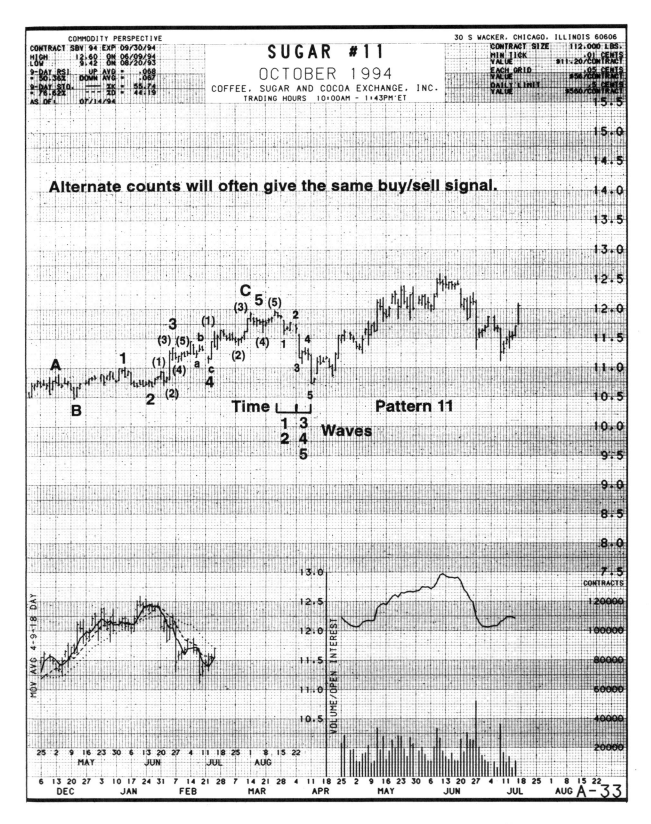

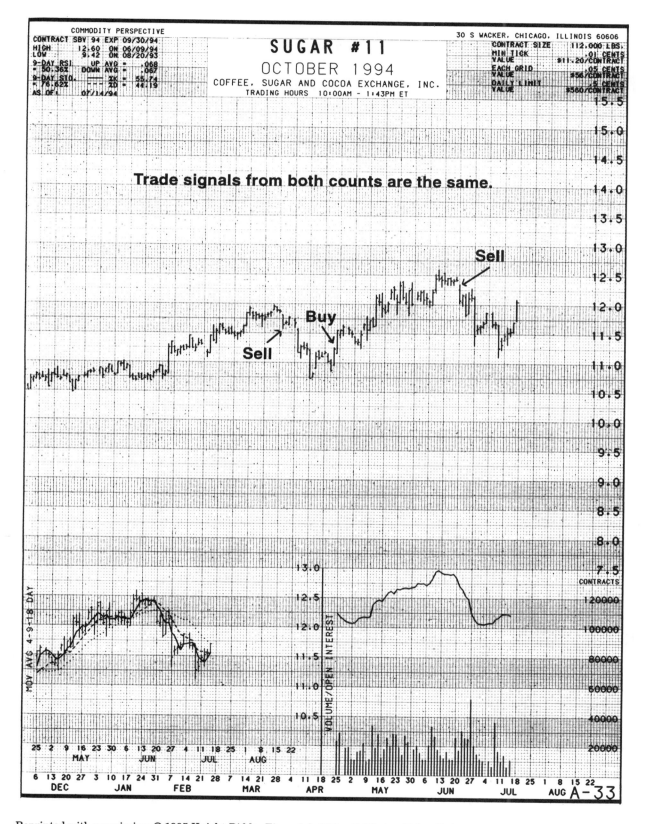

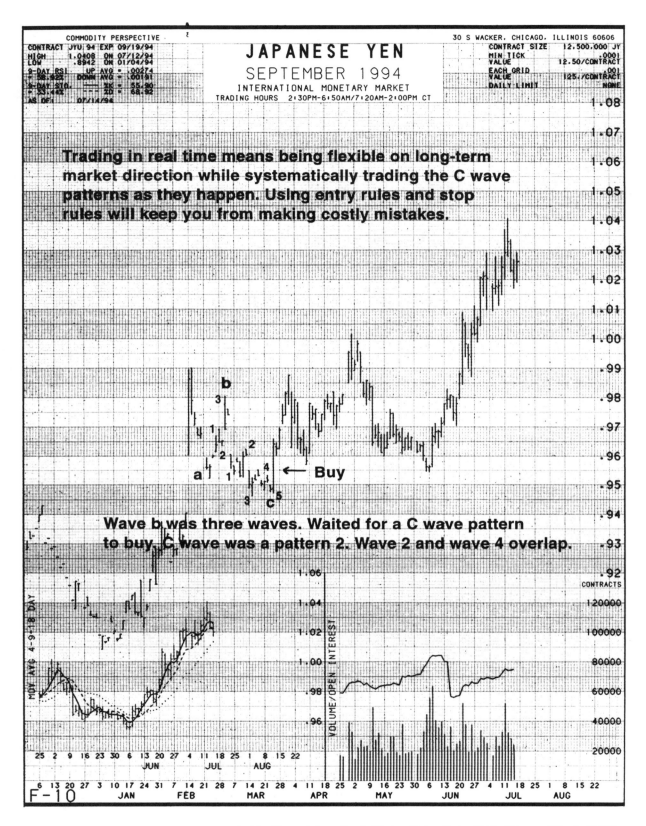

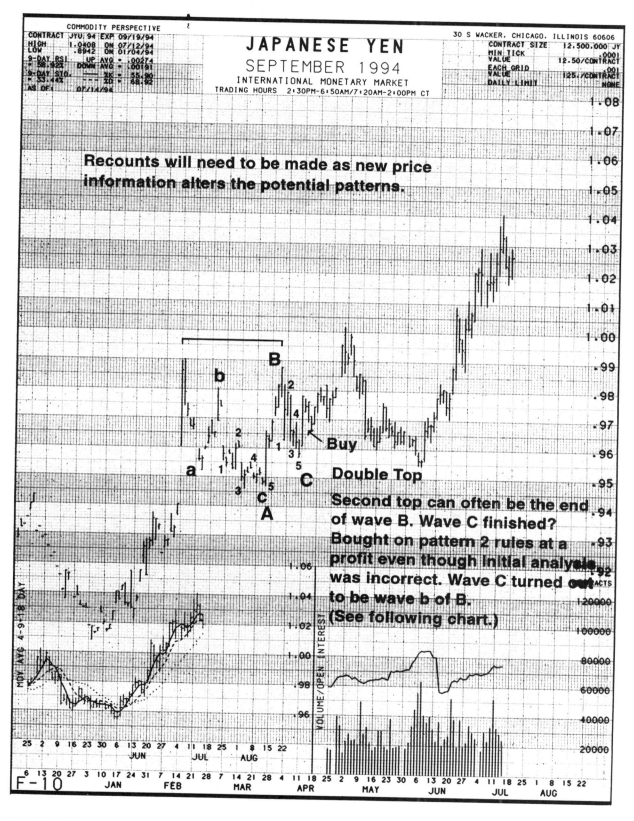

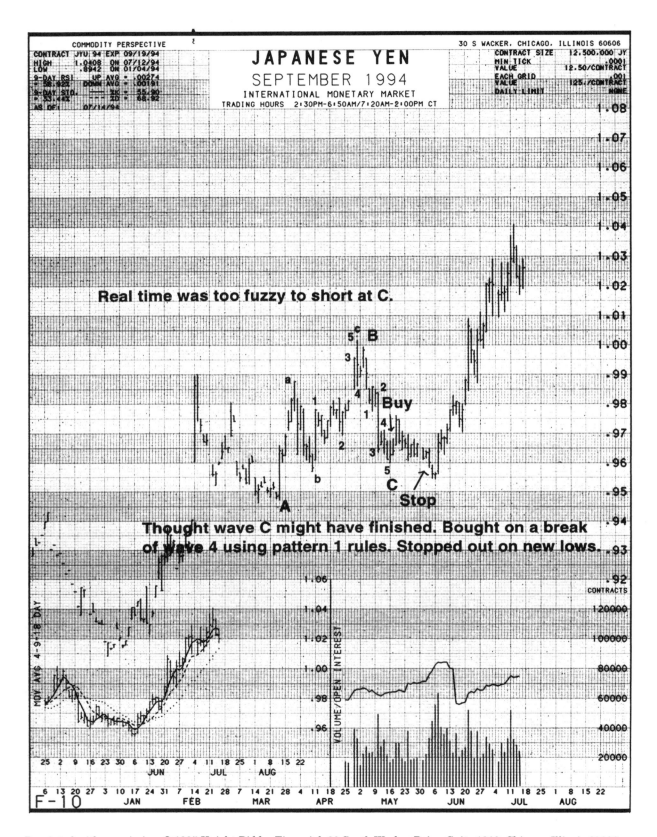

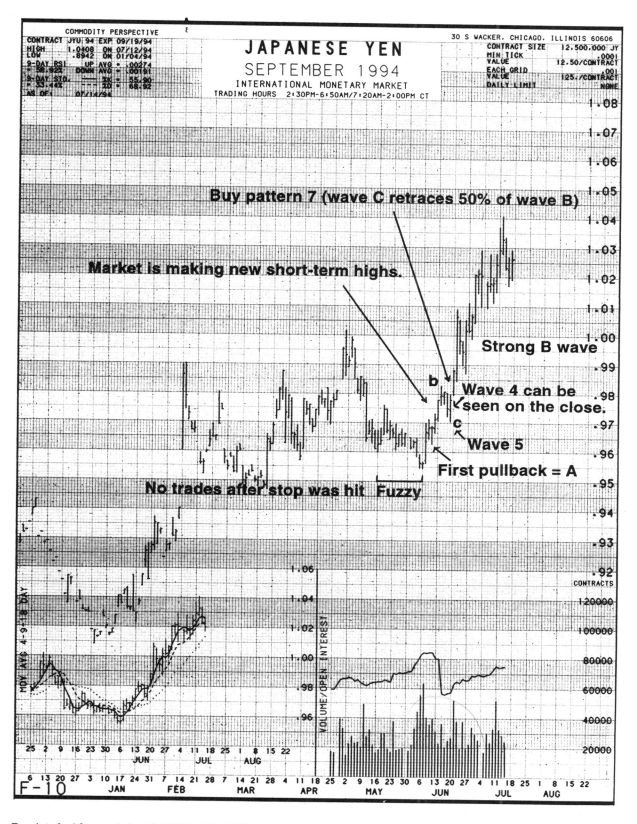

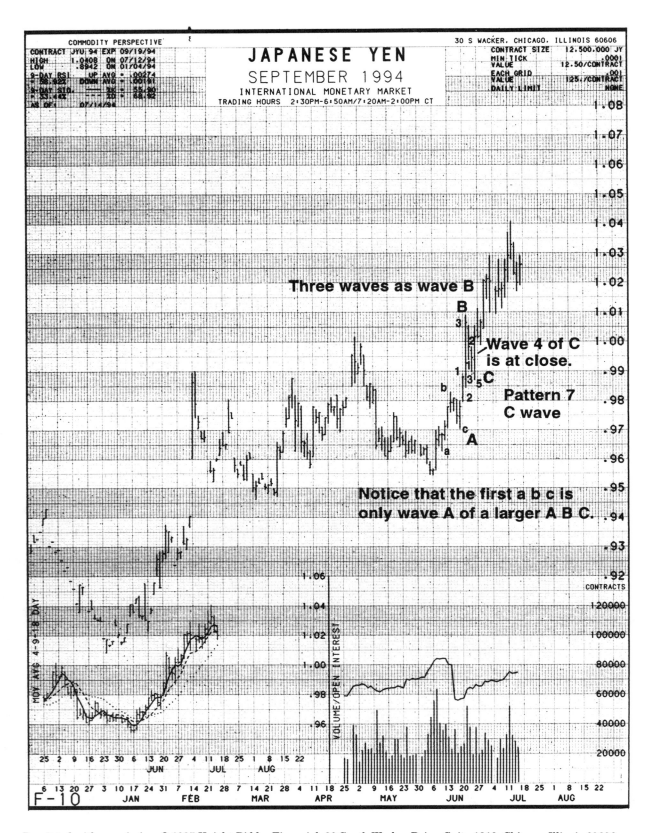

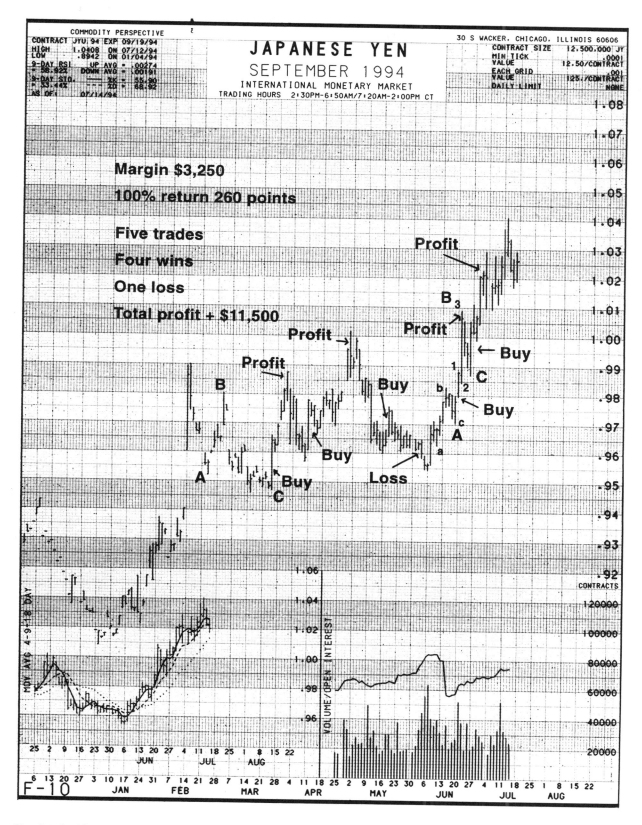

Trading Large C Waves

At this stage, you should understand the phenomenon of large C waves that take the market to new highs or lows (see the diagrams on the next page). This is why you do not always rush to trade opposite the direction of the C wave. Long C waves extend just like impulse moves.

To give you some insight into what I am talking about: Since the 1987 crash, all the stock market advance has been technically corrective in nature. Obviously, there have been more chances to trade on the side of the C wave direction than against it as the market makes new highs. Long term, this indicates a certain structural weakness: When the market eventually turns around, the selloff will be severe. But here you are dealing with a wave degree that is measured in years; realistically, there have been many opportunities to buy the market with smaller C wave patterns. Although this is an extreme example, it happens all the time on a smaller degree and underscores two points:

1. Do not get locked into a view of market direction through your long-term analysis.

2. Trade all the C wave patterns as long as all the rules are met.

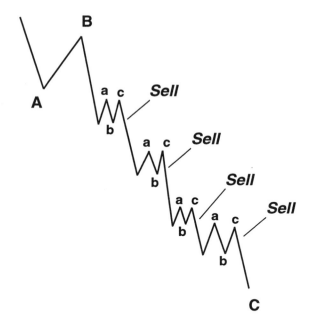

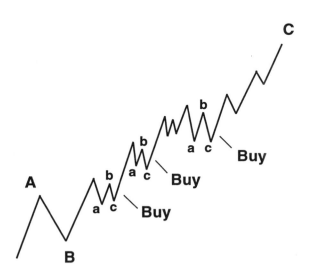

Chapter

9

C Wave Patterns on Daily and Intraday Charts

The following charts are presented for your future reference. The C wave patterns are once again shown in real markets to help you with pattern matching. The profit takes are all fixed targets based on a percentage of margin. These are only guidelines, but they will help you assess this concept's value for yourself.

N.Y. Silver

The following chart of N.Y. Silver over a six-month period shows a long series of a b c corrections. Sometimes the patterns are difficult to decipher—this is when you must stay out of the market. At other times, there are some clear patterns that provide a good easy trade. But when you are in a market with multiple a b c corrections, profit takes must remain relatively small.

The first wave marked is a B wave triangle a b c d e, which then goes on to a wave C. The wave C ends with a pattern 3. The market then declines and makes a double bottom (quite often double bottoms are the start of wave A and the end of wave B). Naturally after this, there will be another C wave. This C wave ended with a pattern 2. Wave 1 and wave 4 overlap.

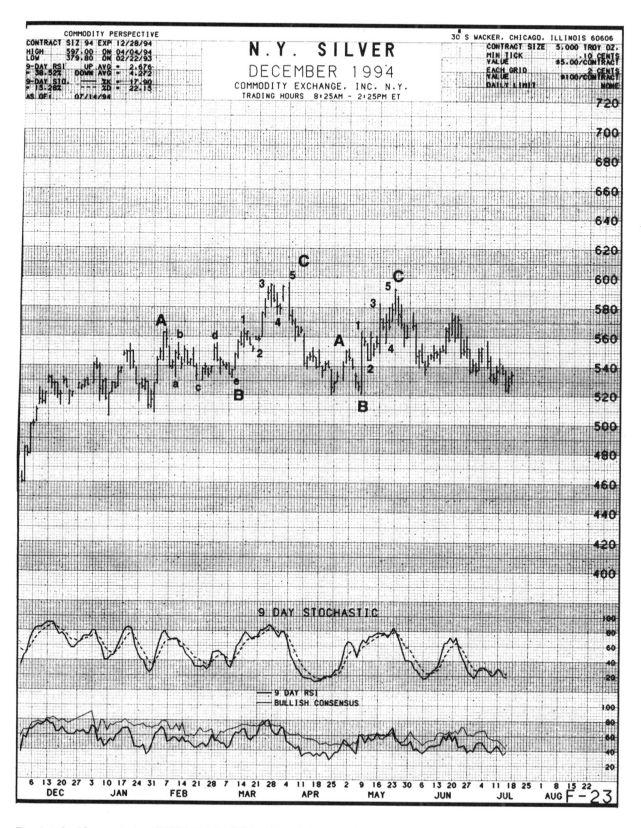

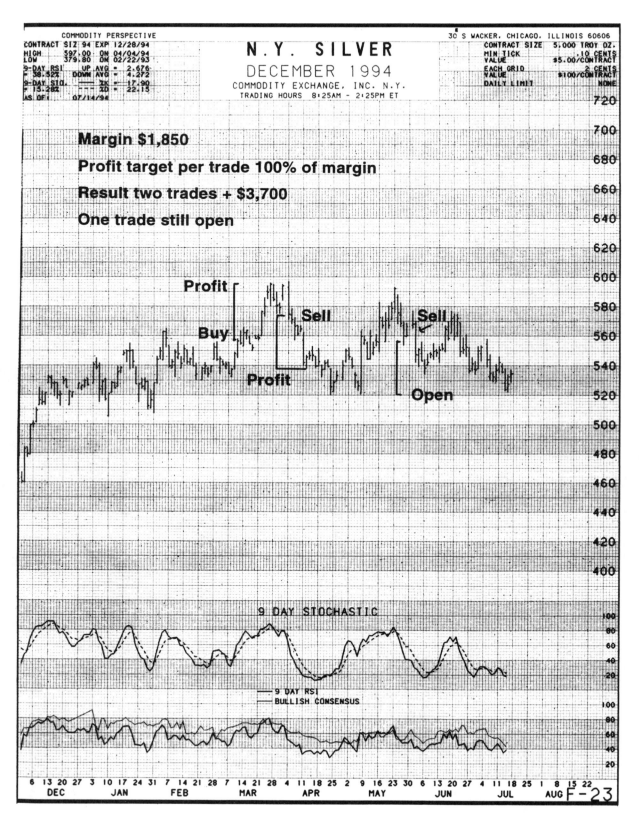

Deutschemark Spot

The Deutschemark Spot chart was used previously (see Chapter 2) to demonstrate a fifth wave triangle. This was the high on the dollar in 1985. Before the fifth wave triangle, I have marked another A B C. This is a good example of a pattern 7, which is a strong B wave with wave a, wave b, wave c, wave d and wave e pulling back into the price area of wave A. The high on the dollar is marked as a strong A B C D E fifth wave triangle. Then after that, the first a b c, which is a small rally on the dollar after it started declining, there was a C wave pattern.

The pattern was a pattern 5, which was just three waves. Looking further, it turns out that the next move down was only three waves after this, meaning that the decline must be a strong B wave. This was followed by an a b c d e, making this a good example of a pattern 6.

Deutschemark—Spot—4 Month

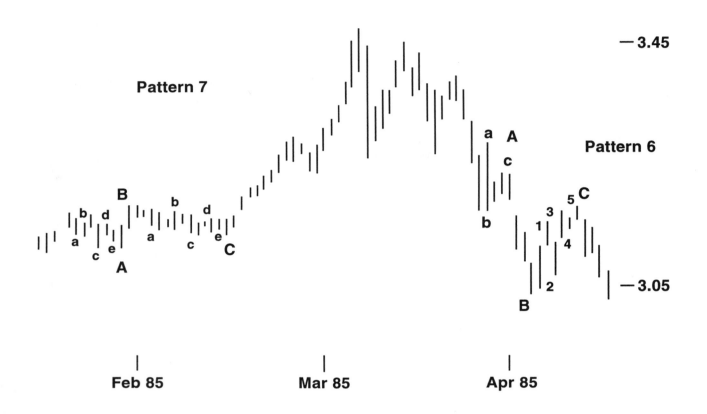

Spot Swiss Franc

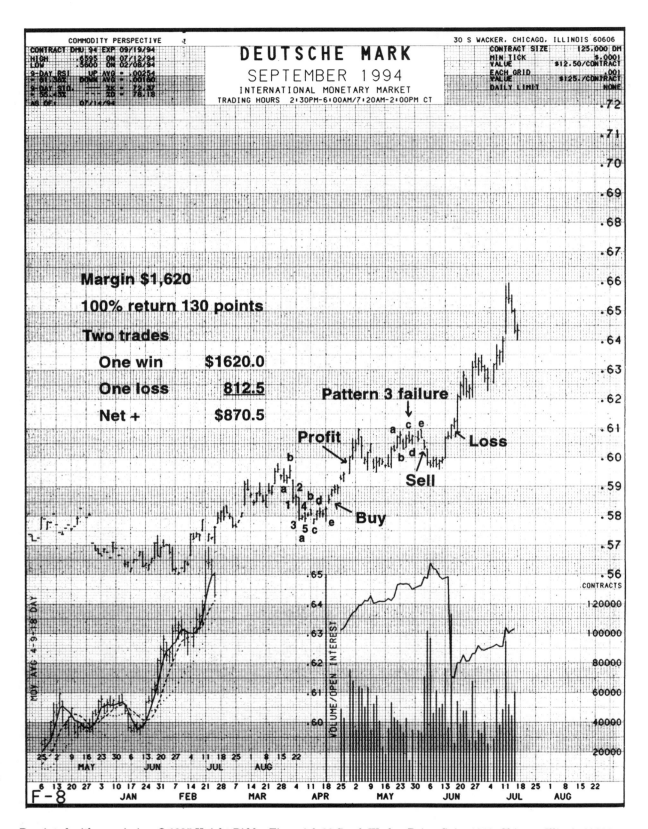

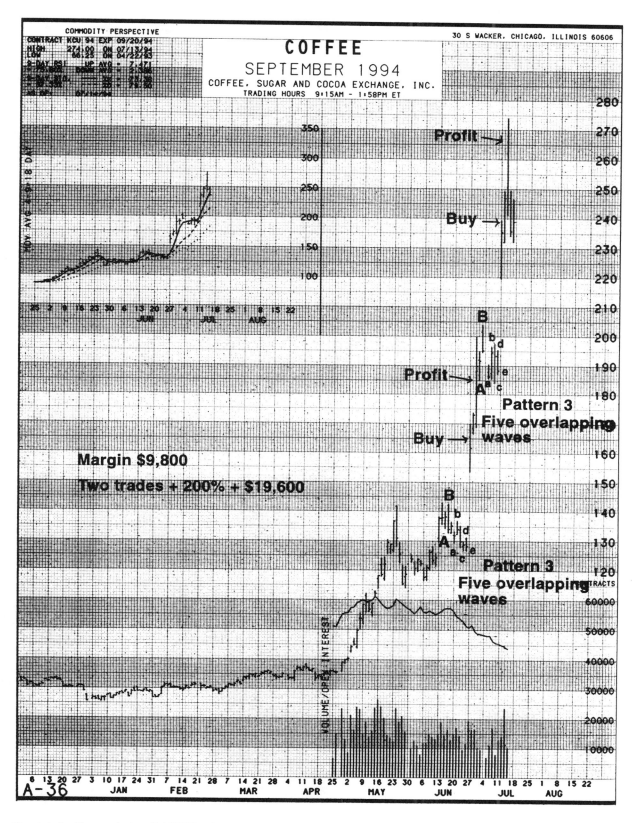

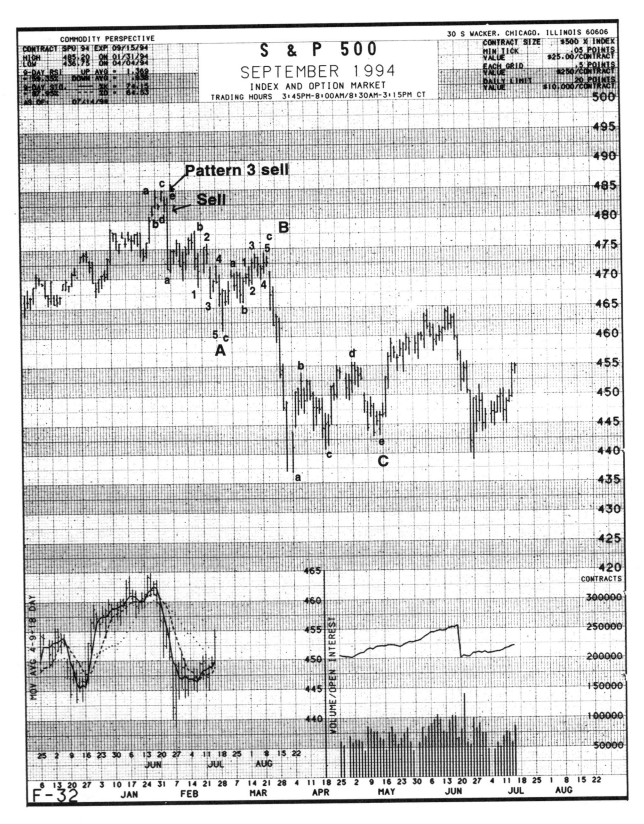

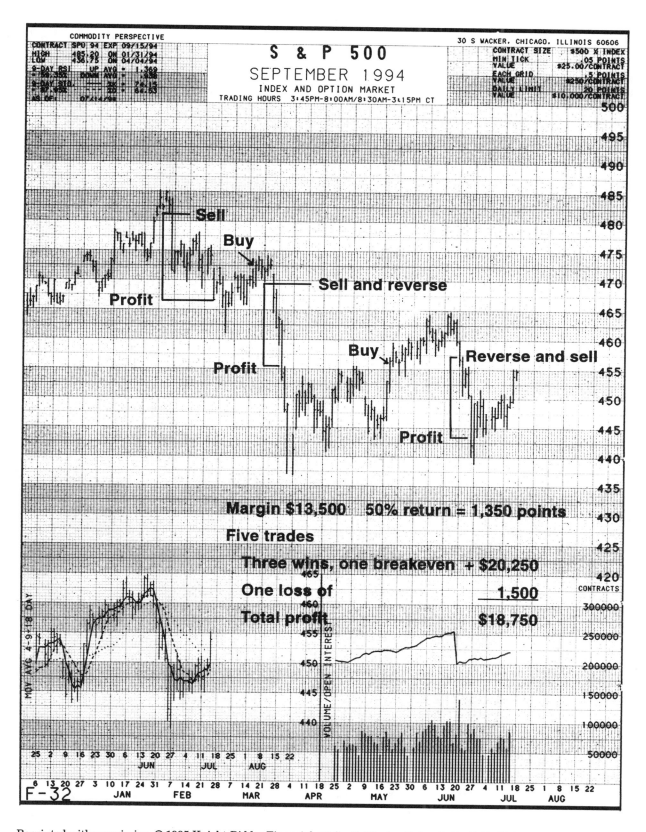

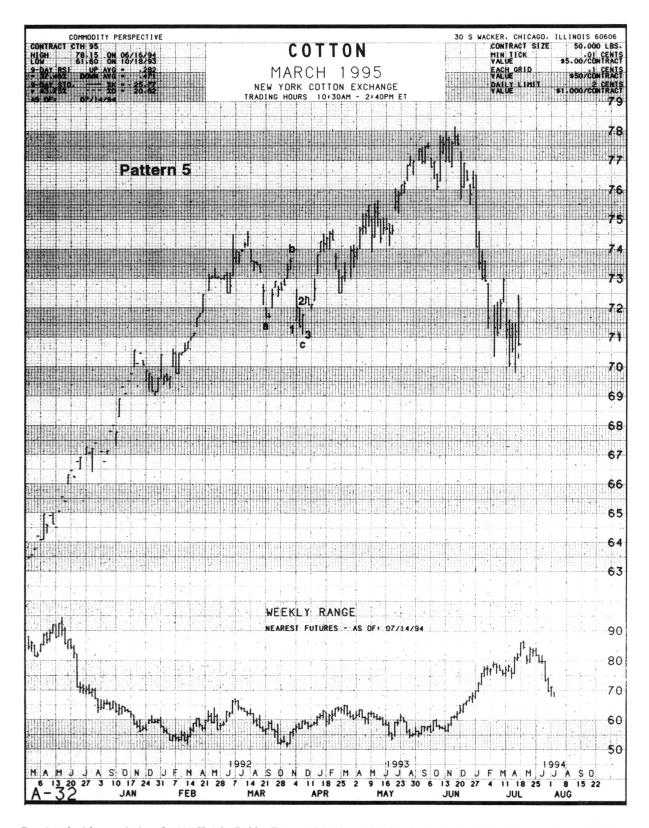

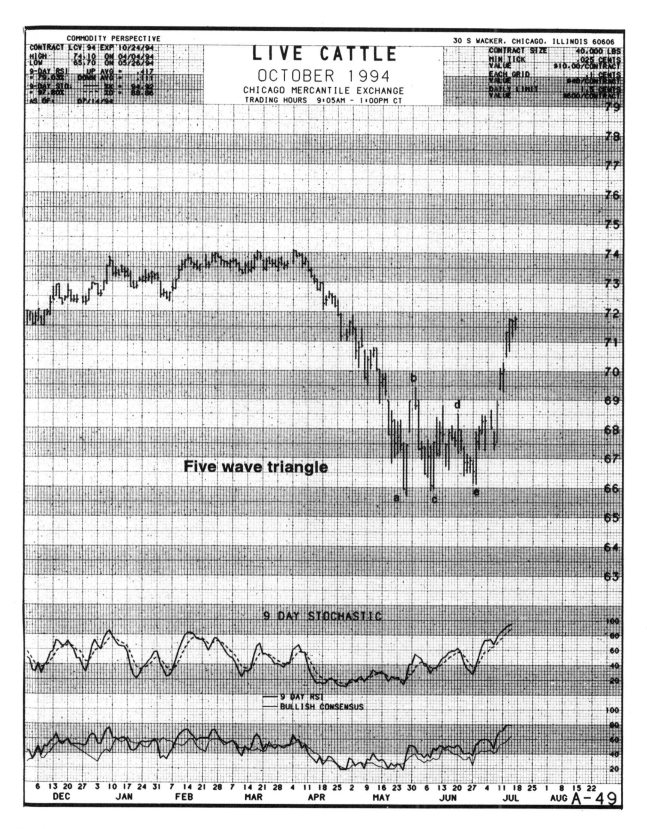

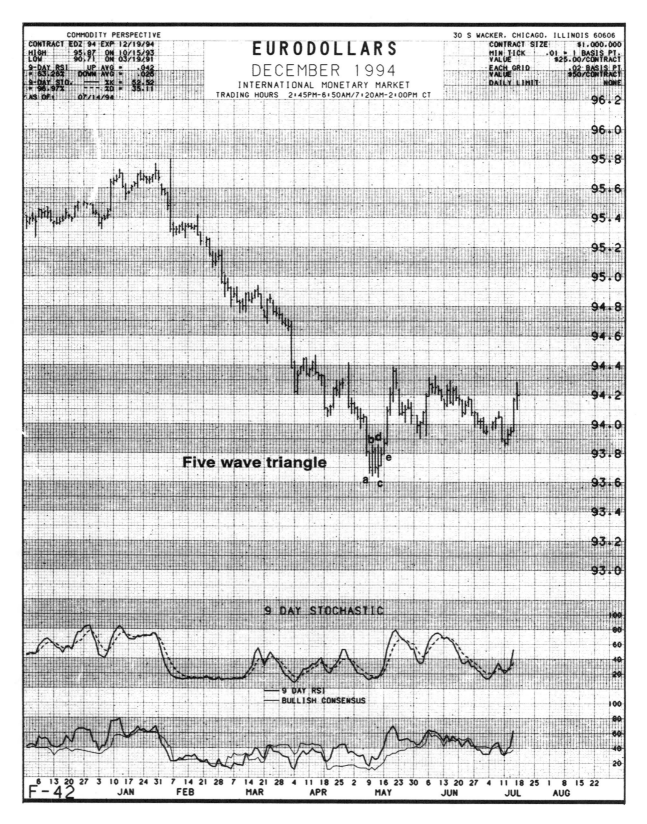

10 Minute Copper

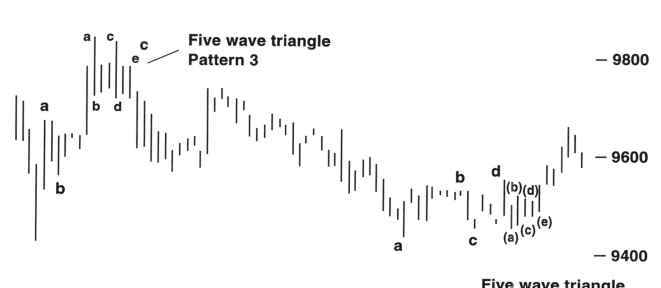

Five wave triangle
Pattern 3

Five wave triangle
ending with a
smaller triangle

S&P 500 60 Minutes

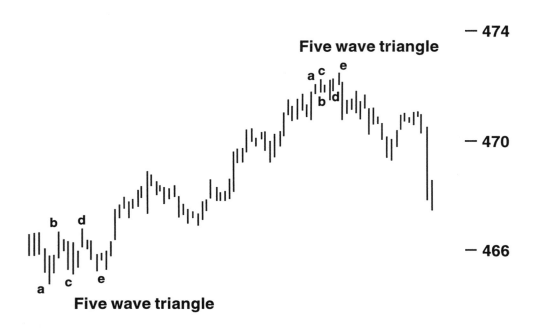

Five wave triangle

Five wave triangle

Copper 120 Minutes

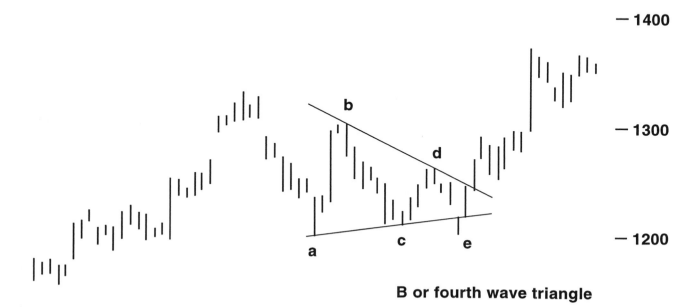

B or fourth wave triangle

**Wave e *sometimes*
breaks the a c trendline.**

**Entry is a break of the
b d trendline or a stop
above/below wave d.**

Deutschemark Hourly

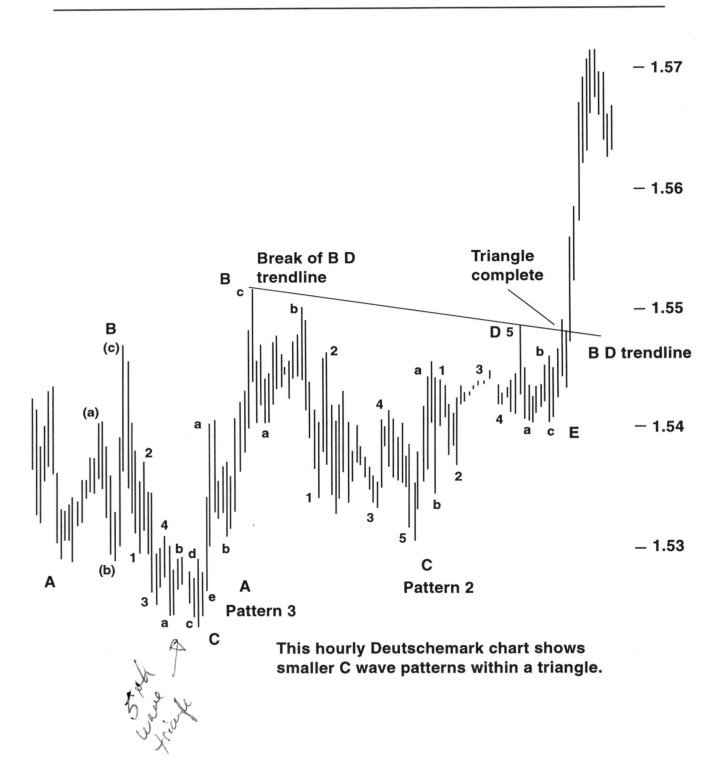

This hourly Deutschemark chart shows smaller C wave patterns within a triangle.

Sugar (CSCE)

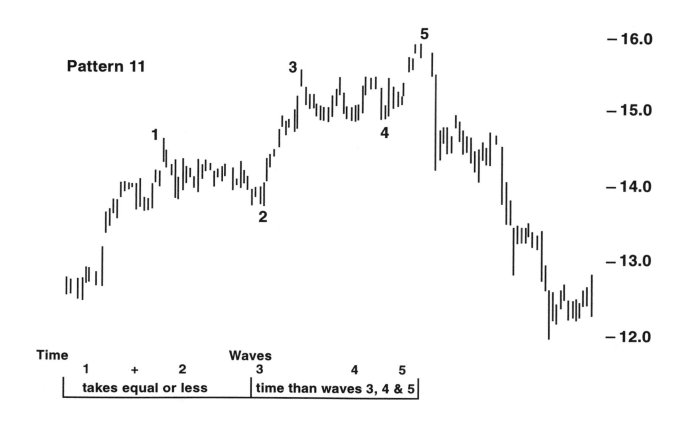

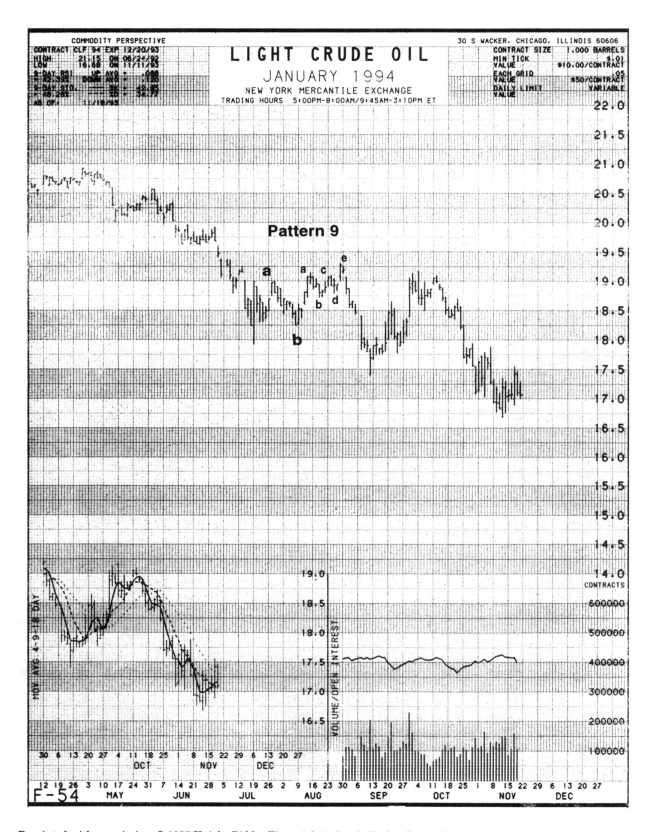

S&P 500 1 Minute

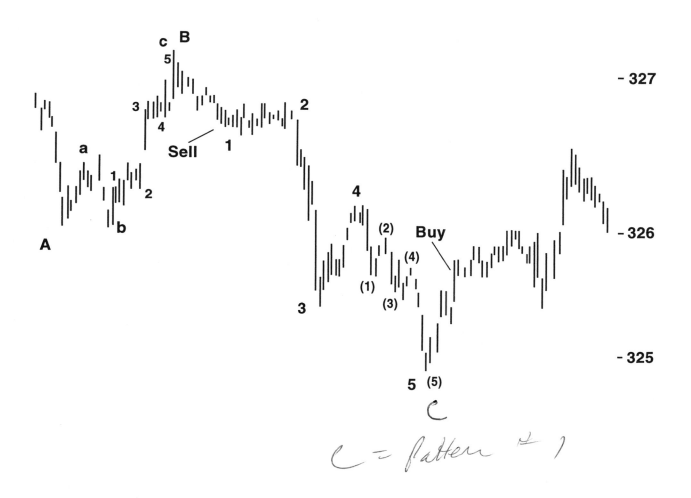

C = pattern # 1

Copper 10 Minutes

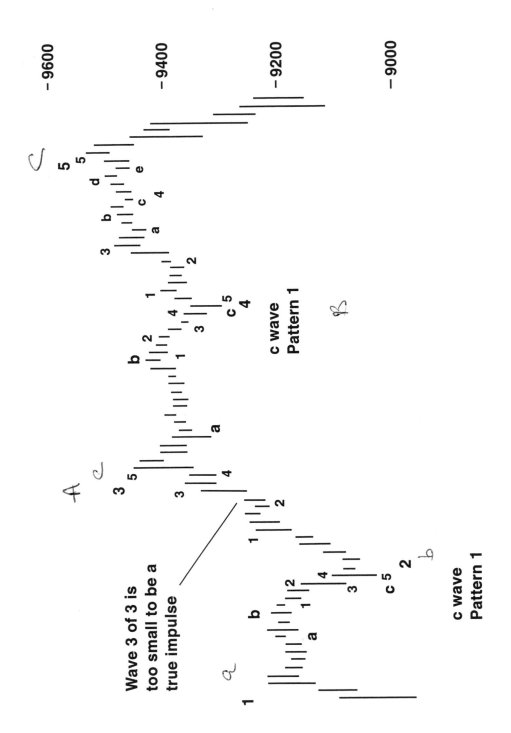

Copper 10 Minutes

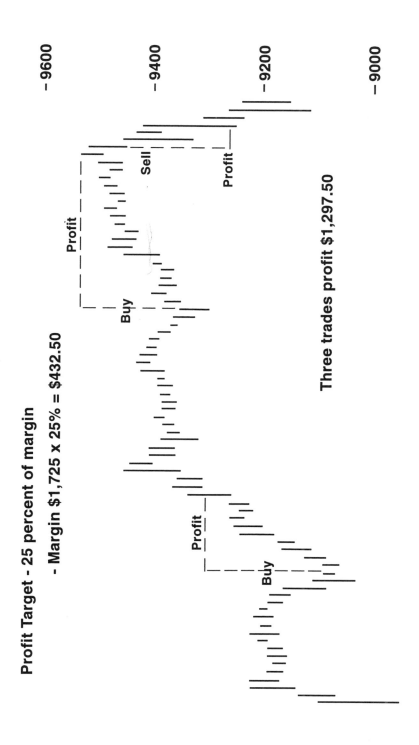

Copper 10 Minutes

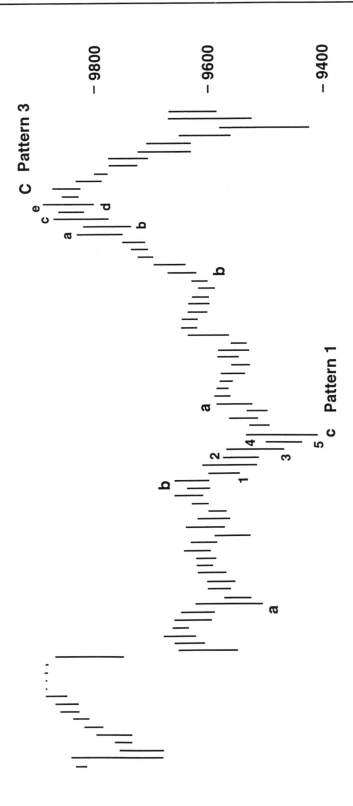

Copper 10 Minutes

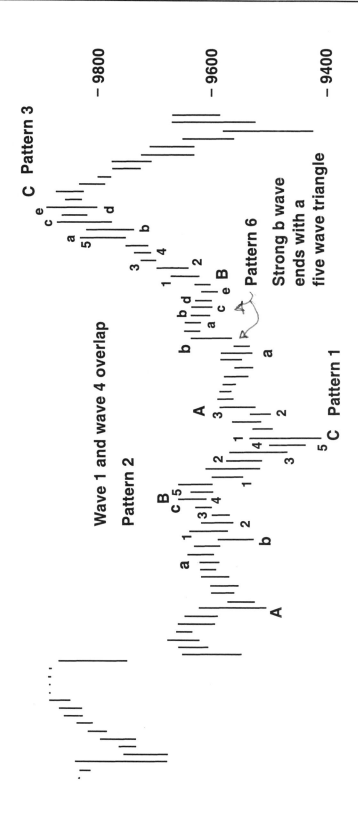

Copper 10 Minutes

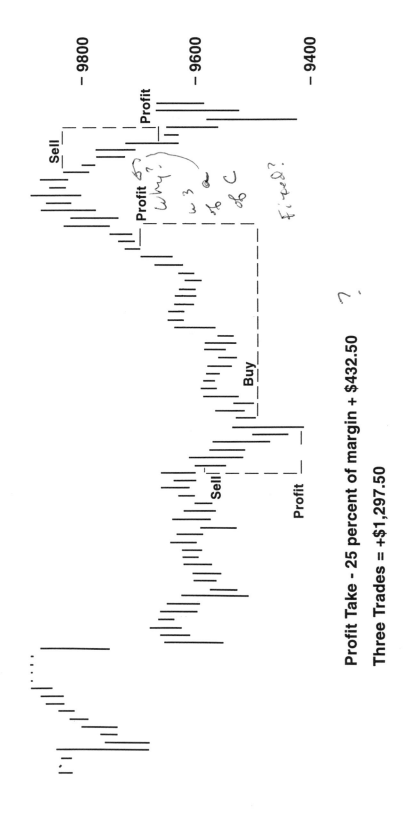

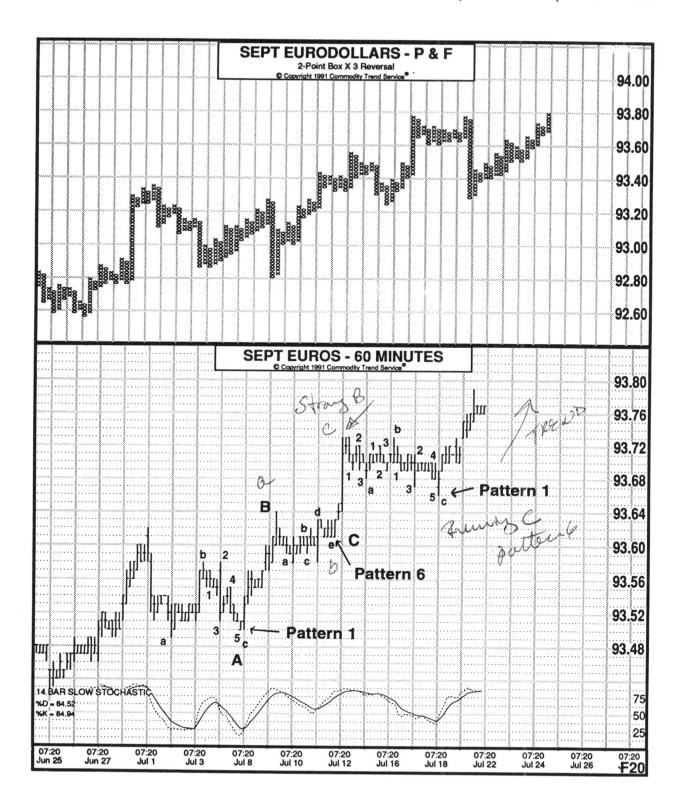

10

C Wave Method in Action

You now know what the C wave patterns look like and how they develop in real time. You can use these patterns in their simplest forms to get short-term trades by matching your price charts with the patterns that I have laid out for you. The full listing of patterns is provided in Chapter 5 for future reference.

Another way to use C wave patterns is to try trend trading in an effort to stay in the trade as long as you can. In this chapter, I will take you through some market action day by day to help you see how this can be done.

1. Draw a line through the midpoint of each day's range to get the general market shape.

2. Mark in a rough count of either (3s) or (5s).

All the price charts used throughout this chapter are reprinted with the kind permission of Bloomberg Financial Markets • Frankfurt 69-920410 • Hong Kong 2-521-3000 • London 171-330-7500 • New York 212-318-2000 • Princeton 609-279-3000 • Singapore 226-3000 • Sydney 2-777-8600 • Tokyo 3-3201-8900 • Washington DC 202-434-1800 • Wellington 499-1765

3. Keep renumbering until you have a logical wave count.

4. Simplify your count by marking the end of every group of waves (5s) or (3s) with a dot and the number of waves in each group.

5. Always mark the first (3) group as a wave A.

6. The next wave group of the same degree is wave B. This may be made up of a smaller a b c (one degree smaller).

7. Any time you have three or more waves on the midpoint chart, try doing detailed counts on the daily charts as well.

8. Keep using both the midpoint and daily charts until you are absolutely sure that wave B has finished.

9. When wave B is complete, the midpoint chart will not be sensitive enough to get an accurate C wave count. Use the daily chart until wave C ends.

10. When your wave count is unclear, check a related market.

11. Place market entry stops only when you have a clear C wave pattern. (See C wave diagrams and rules in Chapter 5.)

12. Once you are in the trade, use the daily charts for stops and a combination of daily and midpoint charts for analysis. Repeat steps 1 to 11.

Entry

The method of entry is the same for every pattern. An entry stop is placed one tick above/below the price bar of wave d or 4. When this stop is activated, a stop loss is placed one tick below/above wave e or 5.

Stops are covered in more detail (see Managing the Trade, later in this chapter).

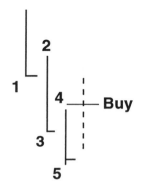

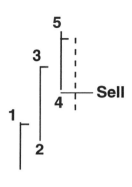

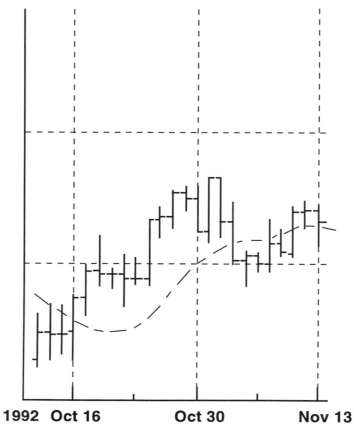

1992 Oct 16   Oct 30   Nov 13

Source: © 1995 Bloomberg Financial Markets

The above chart shows 24 days of data on the OEX (S&P 100). To begin the wave count, draw a line through the midpoint of each day's range to get the general market shape shown below.

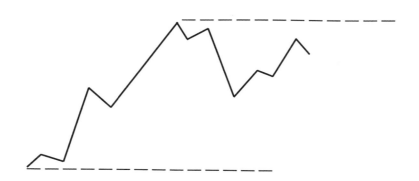

Example 1

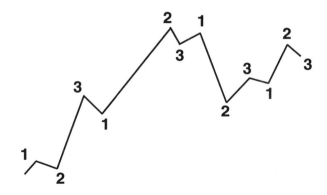

Mark in a rough count of either/or 3s and 5s.

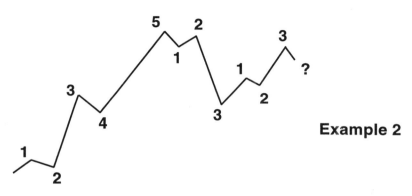

Example 2

Keep renumbering until you have a logical wave count.
Example 2 appears to be the best fit at this point.

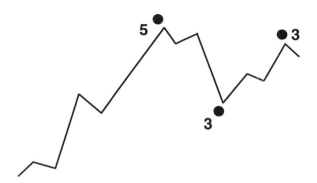

Simplify your count. Mark the end of every group of 5s
or 3s with a dot and the number of waves in each group.

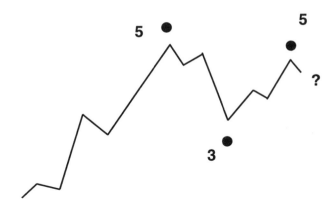

You can say that your first group may be an impulse (5), but you don't know if it is wave 1, wave 3 or wave 5.

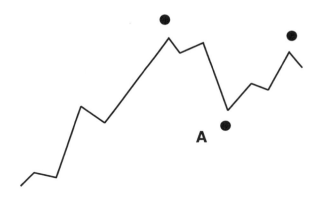

The next group (3) is definitely a correction against the short-term trend (3s are always correction). Therefore, *always mark your first (3) group after a (5) group as A.*

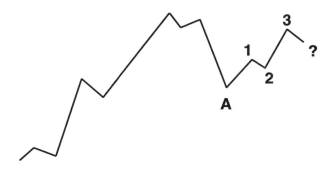

Because you now have a wave A, the next group of 3 or 5 must be wave B. Or if wave B subdivides, the next three groups will be wave B (a) (b) (c). This setup is the most common. It does not affect you either way because your primary interest is wave C.

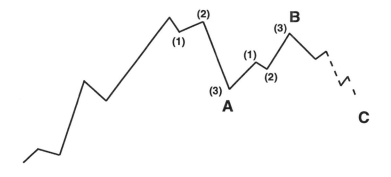

Mark the next group of 3s as wave B.

Now that you have possible wave A and wave B, you must now look for a C wave pattern. You are at the stage where the midpoint method is not sensitive enough to detect the final *five waves* that should *make up wave C*. You now look for five waves on a daily chart by marking in every wave flow (see Counting Waves in Chapter 3).

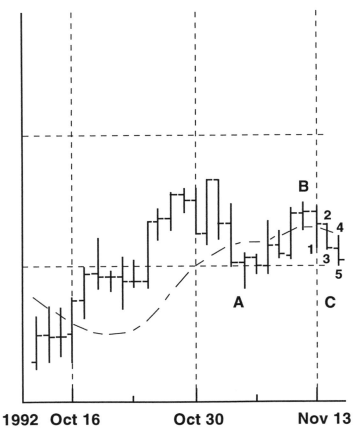

1992 Oct 16   Oct 30   Nov 13

Source: © 1995 Bloomberg Financial Markets

Using the close prices and daily range, you can get a good idea of the wave flow.

Five waves can be counted, but wave 3 does not exceed wave 1. This pattern does not fit into any of our C wave patterns, and the market may expand into the situation as presented in example 2.

Detail of S&P 500 Daily

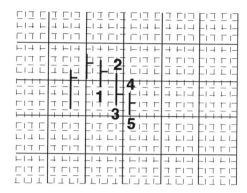

When the wave count is unclear, check a related market. In this case, the S&P 500 shows a clear five wave pattern. Wave 2 and wave 4 do not overlap. Referring to the pattern diagrams and rules, you will find that the C wave on the S&P 500 conforms to the rules of pattern 1.

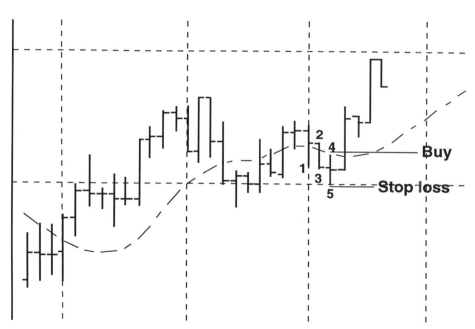

Source: © 1995 Bloomberg Financial Markets

Because you are trading the S&P 100, refer back to the OEX chart and place your entry stop a tick above wave 4 and a stop loss below wave 5.

Managing the Trade

At the beginning of the trade, you cannot do anything until at least three waves have unfolded. Do not use the midpoint method alone to count waves since this method is not sensitive enough. Consider any movement as a wave. When you can count three waves of any degree, your stop can be moved, as in case 1 and case 2.

Case 1

Wave 3 is at least 300 percent in price length when compared to wave 2 (e.g., if wave 2 is 100 points, wave 3 must be 300 points or more). The stop can now be moved up to below wave 2.

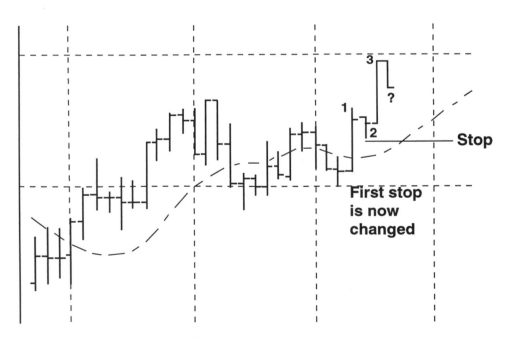

Source: © 1995 Bloomberg Financial Markets

Case 1: Stop moves to below wave 2.

Case 2

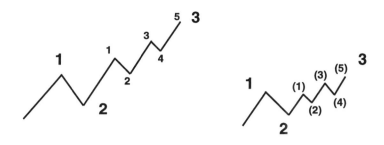

Wave 3 shows five waves.

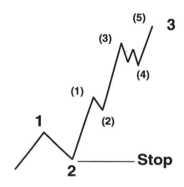

Case 2 (a): If five waves are detected as wave 3, check for an impulse wave. If impulse wave is found, stop is moved to below wave 2.

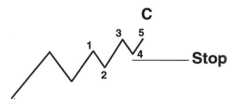

Case 2 (b): Check wave 1 for correction. If wave 1 is corrective, wave 3 will possibly be C wave pattern. If a C wave pattern is confirmed, the stop and reverse is placed below wave 4 of the C wave as usual.

Case 3

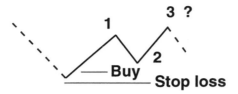

If there is no C wave pattern and wave 3 is less than 300 percent of wave 2, the stop stays in its original place underneath the extreme low.

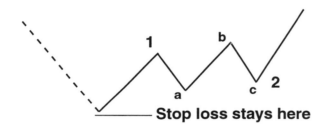

In a situation as described in case 3, wave 3 may turn into wave B.

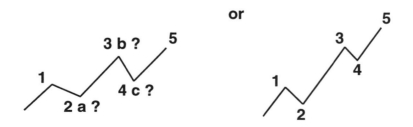

If you are still in the trade, stop points can only be altered when five waves can be counted.

When five waves can be counted, the stop goes under wave 4.

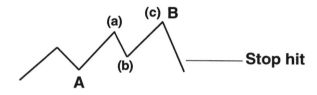

If you get stopped out, check the wave group(s) of wave 5. If they are 3s and not 5s, wave 5 should be renamed wave B.

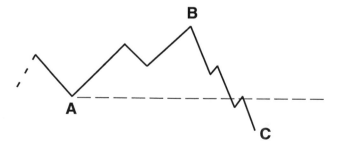

If this is the case, look for a C wave pattern. Do not attempt to stay in the trade. This C wave may retrace all the previous price moves and more.

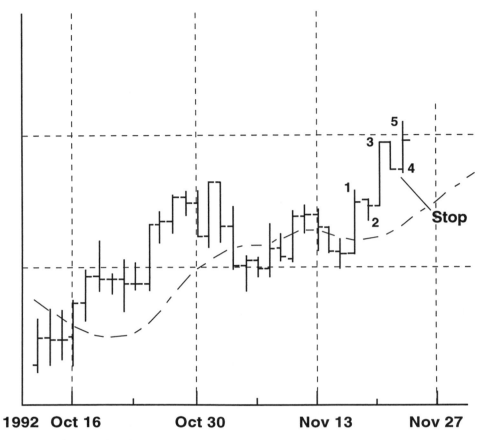

Source: © 1995 Bloomberg Financial Markets

Five waves can now be counted. The stop is moved from below wave 2 and is now placed below wave 4.

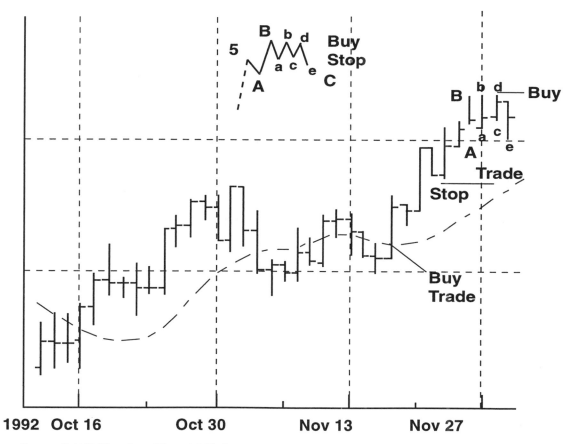

Source: © 1995 Bloomberg Financial Markets

Because the assumed wave B is so strong compared to wave A, this is looking like pattern 6, 7 or 8 (see pattern rules in Chapter 5). The stop to enter the market goes above wave d with a stop loss below wave e. You still maintain your original position with the stop loss below wave 4.

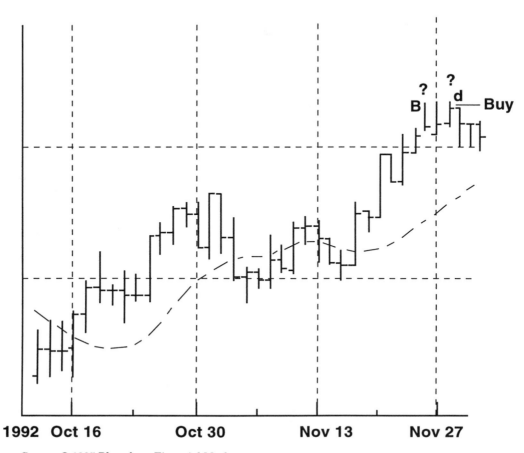

Source: © 1995 Bloomberg Financial Markets

The stop to enter the market above wave d has not been hit, and the market has continued to correct (sideways markets are corrective). This calls for a recount. Wave A is still straight forward, but wave B may be incorrect.

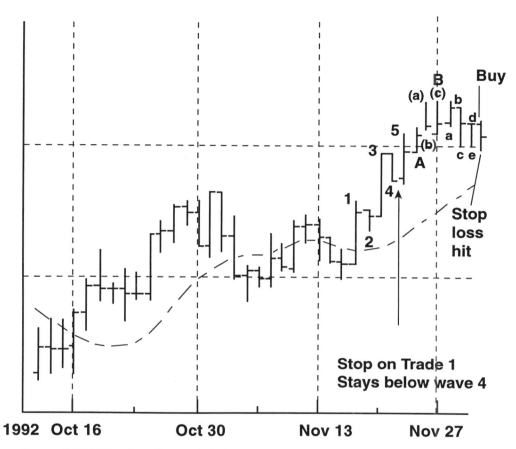

Source: © 1995 Bloomberg Financial Markets

Strictly using the entry rules, you were stopped into the market a tick above wave d. That same day your stop loss was hit a tick below wave e. Wave B is still obviously strong compared to wave A so any C wave must be a pattern 6, 7 or 8. A new buy stop was placed above the high of the day.

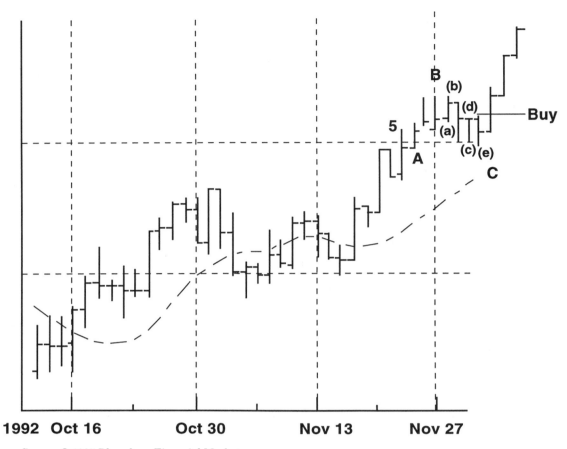

Source: © 1995 Bloomberg Financial Markets

You have been successfully stopped into a pattern 7 trade.

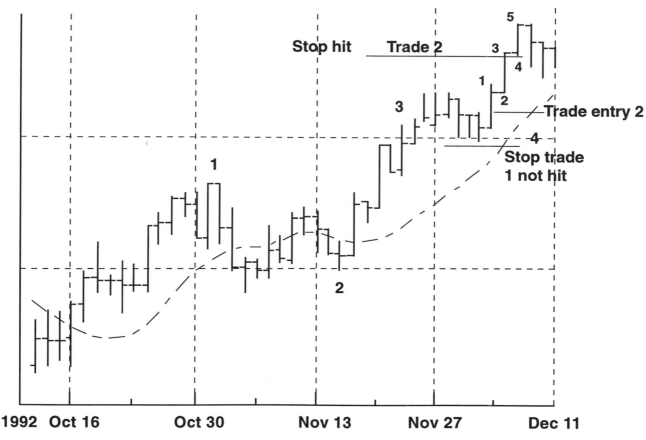

Source: © 1995 Bloomberg Financial Markets

The stops on trade 2 have been progressively raised from below entry to under wave 2 and then raised again to under wave 4. The stop under wave 4 was then hit, leaving just your original open position. Marked on the chart are complete wave groups that make up the larger waves 1, 2, 3 and 4.

The stop rules are used on the large wave groups in the same manner as the smaller groups. You are always trying to cut your risk, and you achieve this by moving stops up on new positions using smaller degree waves.

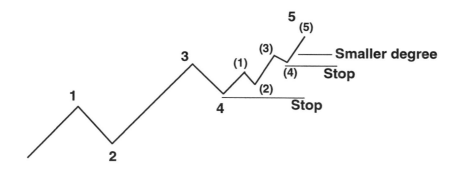

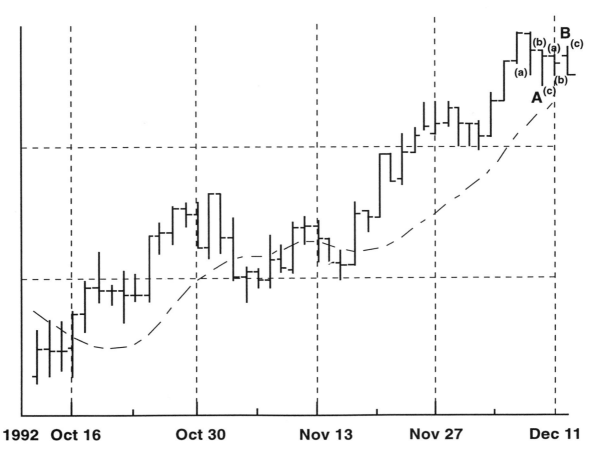

Wave A and wave B have finished.

Now look for the C wave pattern.

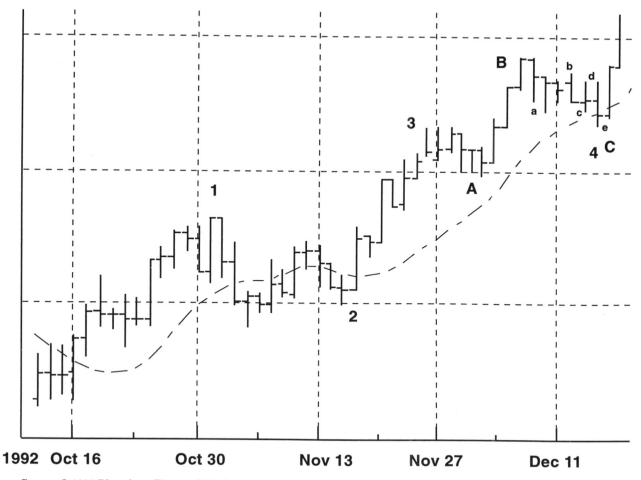

Notice that the wave marked B is 5 waves; this was previously labeled wave 5. In fact, it was wave B of a pattern 6 A B C running correction.

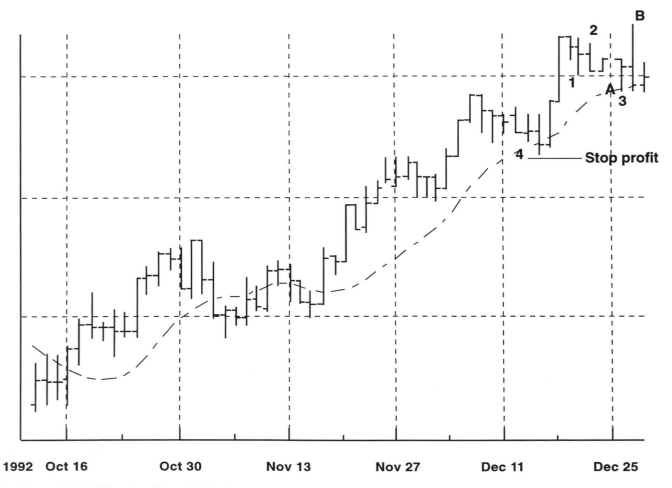

Source: © 1995 Bloomberg Financial Markets

Your stop profit stays below wave C of wave 4.

Profit takes and reversals can only be made if wave 5 becomes pattern 3, or a clear five waves.

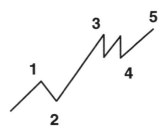

The last day of trading has broken the pattern 3 range. Wave A is a correction.

Rule: First (3) is wave A.

This alone suggests that the downmove is not a change of trend. But on the other hand, you do not know how far the C wave will carry you. It would be quite possible to retrace the complete upmove. Now that you have wave A and wave B, you are looking for a C wave pattern.

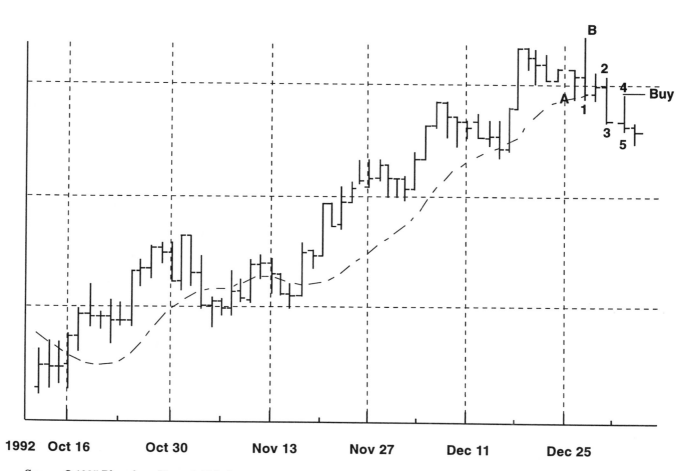

Source: © 1995 Bloomberg Financial Markets

Wave C now has a five wave pattern 2.

The entry stop goes above wave 4.

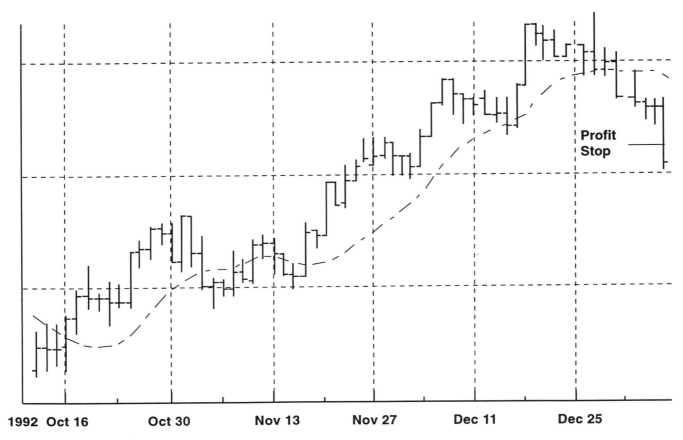

Source: © 1995 Bloomberg Financial Markets

Your stop profit was hit, and you wait on the sidelines. Wave C has become too complex on the OEX, so you use the cash S&P to help with the count.

(For clarity, this S&P 500 chart was constructed from a daily chart using high/low and close prices to get the correct wave flow. It is not a midpoint chart.)

Rule: Check related markets to clarify the count.

S&P 500

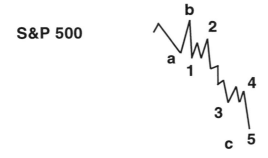

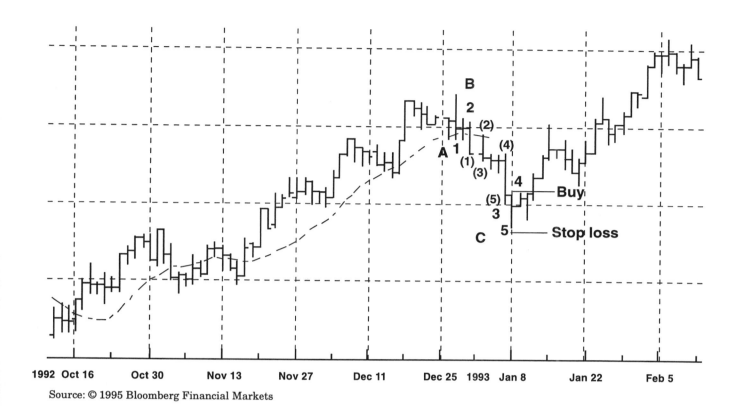

Source: © 1995 Bloomberg Financial Markets

Wave C obeys the rules of pattern 1. Now refer back to the OEX chart, and place a stop above wave 4 to enter a new position with a stop loss beneath wave 5.

Now let's take a look at a second example of market action playing out day by day.

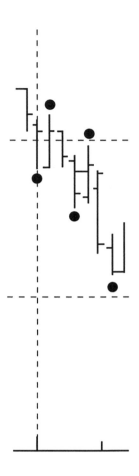

Eight days of May wheat are illustrated above. Since you have a wave group of at least three waves on the midpoint (more in this case), you can try a detailed daily wave flow.

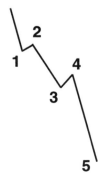

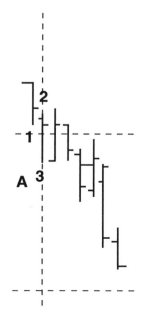

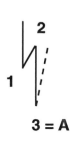

3 = A

The daily wave count is clear enough to use. Wave 1 is a (3), therefore, it is marked wave A.

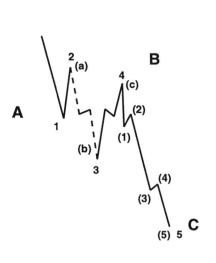

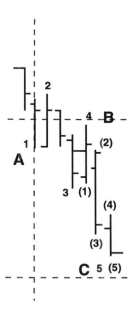

The next part is fuzzy until wave 4 overlaps wave 1 and on day 7 the market closed down. Wave 4 is wave (c) of B. You are now looking for a C wave pattern.

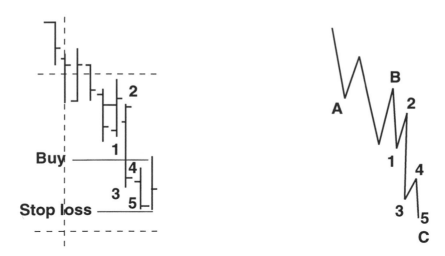

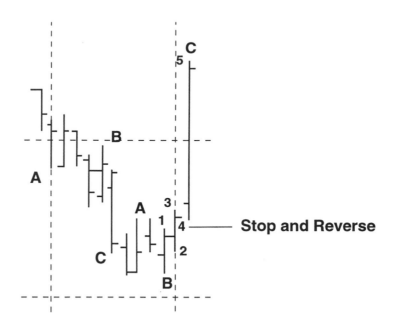

Wave C is a pattern 1. Our entry stop above wave 4 was hit, and you are now long with a stop under wave 5. The market then went sideways. Your stop below wave 5 was not hit. Above is a wave flow that shows the real wave count. This does not alter your long position in any way.

There is a clear double bottom that now can be labeled wave A and wave B. Wave 5 of wave C is very long when compared to both wave A and wave B and also when compared to wave 1 and wave 3 of wave C. Wave C is elongated. Your stop and reverse goes under wave 4.

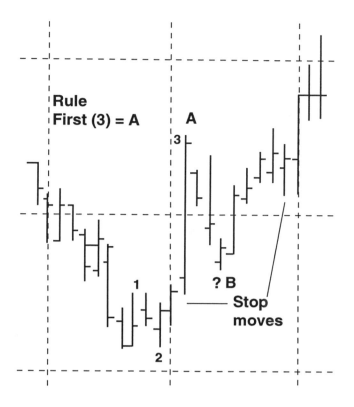

Your stop *has not* been hit, and you have not found any C wave patterns to add on with. The wave count is murky, so you are now using both the midwave and daily charts for your wave counts.

Stop losses should now be raised.

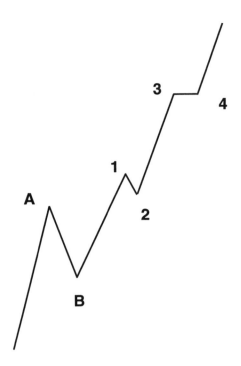

The midpoint provides the clearest look at the market. Wave B has ended, and you are looking for a clear C wave pattern on the daily chart. Now you will experiment and see if you can get a good fit on your wave count.

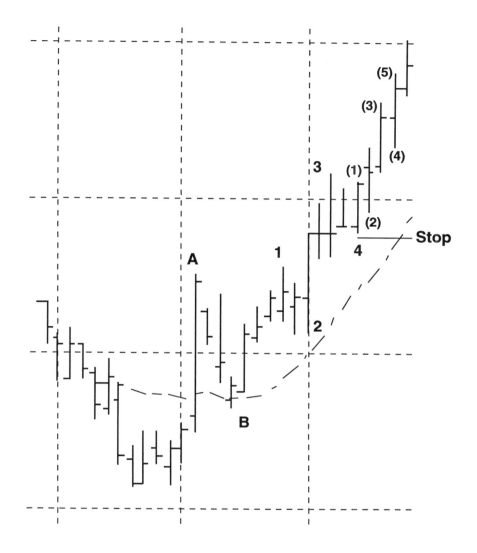

In all honesty, the last wave (5) is subdividing so much that it is hard to get a good count. Unless this ends with a pattern 3, I can see no way of entering the market as a seller (profit and reverse). You must raise your stop to take profits now that you have a clear wave 4. But if the market were to pass through here now without a pattern 3 signal, you would have to stand aside. Remember, unless the pattern is clear, conserve your capital for a better opportunity.

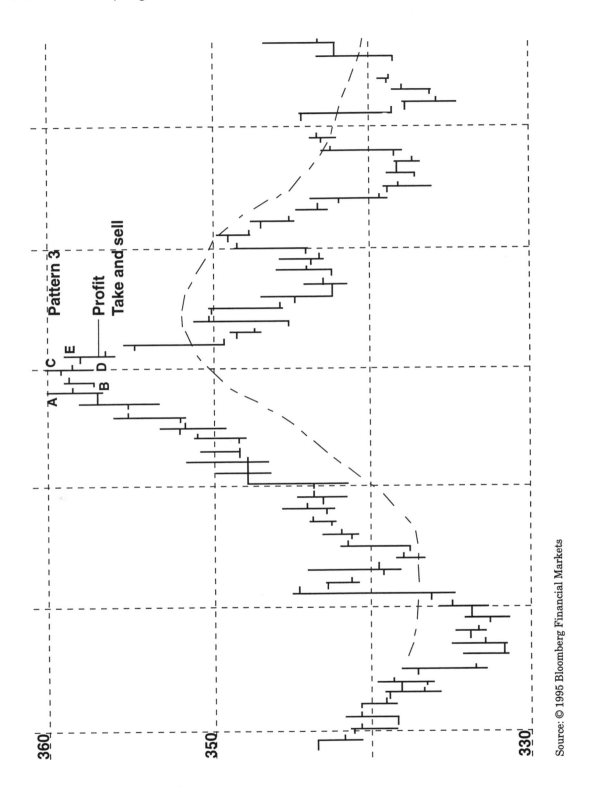

The pattern 3 is quite clear so you could move your stop up to below wave D. There you took profits as well as reversed your position.

Conclusion

After working through the previous examples, you can see how relatively easy a complex subject can become. You will note that you made profitable trades without getting caught up in any long-term wave counts. It is not necessary to have a deep knowledge of the Elliott Wave Principles to make profits as long as you pay attention to detail and make sure that you follow the C wave pattern recognition rules. The experience that you need for long-term counts will come with time, but even then you must realize that Elliott Wave is an indicator of future events and only offers the most probable outcome—new information enters the market, the wave structure will adapt. For this reason, never have a view on the market and keep your wave counts up-to-date.

Summary

It is with good reason that the Elliott Wave Theory has retained the interest of traders for more than 60 years. Elliott Wave is one of the few market methods that can effectively identify where the current price belongs in the overall structure of the market. With this information, a trader can decide whether to be buying dips or selling the rally. The C wave patterns have taken Elliott's wave principles to a new level of precision and as such are a significant breakthrough for real time traders. There should be no need to look at the market in hindsight. The C wave patterns will get you on the right side of the market, whether the moves are large or small.

You must be prepared to take the time to study and match the C wave patterns every market day. Consistency is the key. If you can do this, you will never miss a good trade again. This is a discipline that requires constant application, but the rewards are many.

Fibonacci in a Nutshell

The Fibonacci ratios and Elliott Wave are bound to gether in the public mind as one, but Elliott originally conceived the wave theory without any knowledge that the Fibonacci sequence existed. The C wave patterns also stand alone outside any other market technical inputs such as moving averages, relative strength indexes. However, you do not have to abandon other technical studies. When you get a reliable signal from another type of system, you can always increase your trading size.

Consider the Fibonacci ratios only as an indicator. If you do not find any price or time ratios, do not let that stop you from taking the trade when you have a C wave signal.

The Fibonacci sequence is made up like this,

1 + 2 = 3

   2 + 3 = 5

      3 + 5 = 8

         5 + 8 = 13

            8 + 13 = 21

and so on into infinity.

The Fibonacci ratios used in market calculations are expressed in percentage terms as follows:

    38.2 %

    61.8 %

    138.2 %

    161.8 %

    238.2 %

    261.8 %

This is how it works in theory: Say that the market has moved up 100 points and is now pulling back. You would look to buy when the market is at

62 points   that is 100 − 38.2 points

38 points   that is 100 − 61.8 points

or if wave 1 was 100 points and wave 2 was 40 points, you would look to sell wave 3 at the different Fibonacci ratio points. These are calculated by adding them to the end of wave 1 (which in this case is 100 points).

The Fibonacci ratios would give the following sell points.

sell at 138 = (100 x 38.2% + 100)

         162 = (100 x 61.8% + 100)

         238 = (100 x 138.2% + 100)

         262 = (100 x 161.8% + 100)

         338 = (100 x 238.2% + 100)

         362 = (100 x 261.8% + 100)

You can see the problem: There are now so many sell points that it would be foolish to use the ratios by themselves as a method for finding a target. It is quite likely that the market will reverse for a while from around one of these points, but the risks of selling at these ratio targets outweigh the gains. More rewarding is using the ratios to predict the likely termination time of a correction. Fibonacci time targets are calculated the same way as price. Take the time of wave A and wave B when added together, and multiply them by the Fibonacci ratios. For instance, if wave A and wave B when added together equal 10 time periods, your time targets for the end of wave C are 4, 6, 14, 16, 24 and 26 time periods.

I can not stress this point enough: At this stage, the Fibonacci ratios are only an indicator and remain so until a definitive set of rules can be discovered that will enable them to be used with consistency in the real world of trading.

When a C wave pattern
Completes at a Fibonacci — Good signal

Appendix

II

Daily Worksheet

When counting waves, the practiced trader puts in a lot of work—almost subconsciously.

Using a *daily worksheet*, you can lay out logically the complete analytical process so that, by following all the steps, you will always arrive at the best answer. In following this process, you become a detective—putting together the clues that tell you where and when the next market move will happen. The daily worksheet will save you considerable time even after you become proficient at Elliott Wave counts. This checklist lays out every step so that no potential clue can be overlooked. You may want to photocopy the worksheet for ease of use.

No matter what type of trading you do, always look at charts of one higher degree than you normally use. If you trade in intraday, do a preliminary wave count using the daily charts. If you use daily charts, look at the weekly and monthly charts. This preliminary count does not need to be strictly accurate on this initial glance, but it does serve to remind you of the type of market that you are in and therefore lend a sense of perspective.

If you are trading currencies or stock market futures that are trending in nature, you must eventually do long-term wave counts using monthly charts. But if you are trading markets such as live cattle, which obviously oscillate in price bands, there is no point in trying to do long-term counts when the most useful application of Elliott Wave is on daily charts.

When using the worksheet, circle the + or − signs so that you have a quick reference of the work that you have already done. The more + signs that you have, the more likely that your analysis is correct. Mark your investigative ideas under comments to keep them fresh in your mind.

Daily Worksheet

Wave 1

+   –   Can you count five waves (three in the direction of the trend, two corrective)?

+   –   Do the two corrective waves show alternation?

+   –   Is the alternation in the form of price?

+   –   Is the alternation in the form of wave structure (e.g., the first may be an a b c, the second an a b c d e, or the first may be a flat, the second may be a zigzag)?

+   –   Is the alternation in the form of time? For instance, correction 1 may be five days, correction 2 noticeably longer or shorter. Also at this point, check for Fibonacci time ratios between the first and second corrections (e.g., the first correction took ten days, the second took six days, therefore correction 2 is approximately 61.80 percent of correction 1).

+   –   Are there any Fibonacci time ratios between correction 1 and correction 2? If there is no alternation between correction 1 and 2, you might be in a corrective zigzag pattern.

Zigzags often act the same way as an impulse. For practical purposes at this stage, treat the move as impulsive until there is more evidence. Wave 1 may be extending, and the move may be showing power because of some strong underlying fundamental considerations that you are as yet unaware of.

+   –   When comparing the three waves that move in the direction of the new trend, is one of these waves longer than the other two?

If the waves are all similar in price, note that they may possibly be a zigzag and not the start of a new impulse move.

+   –   When comparing the three waves that move in the direction of the new trend, is the middle wave longer in price than at least one of the other waves?

If the middle wave is the shortest, this move is a correction.

If you believe that you are in wave 1 and you can count only three waves before wave 4 enters the price area of wave 1, you are now in wave B of a correction.

Comments: _____

_____

_____

_____

_____

_____

_____

Wave 2

+ − Is wave 2 a correction of at least a simple A B C?

+ − Compared to wave 1, does wave 2 take a least one-third of the amount of time to complete (e.g., wave 1 took ten periods to complete, wave 2 must take at least three periods)?

+ − Has wave 2 retraced more than 99 percent of wave 1? If so, this is definitely not wave 2. You must either be in wave B of a correction and the wave that you have labeled as wave 1 was a zigzag not an impulse, or your count is totally incorrect in which case you will need to go through the whole process again from at least three waves back.

+ − Does wave A subdivide into three smaller waves?

+ − Does wave B subdivide into three smaller waves?

+ − Does wave C subdivide into five smaller waves? If this happens, there is a strong chance that wave 2 is now complete and you should take any entry signal in the direction of the trend.

If at this point a five wave triangle occurs with every wave clearly subdivided, you are in wave B not wave 2. The exception to this is intraday currencies where you will often see that wave 2 on a 120-minute chart is a small triangle. Wave 2 can often be a running correction during strong impulsive markets. Wave A, wave B and wave C will be corrective, so there should be no confusion.

Comments: _____

_____

_____

_____

_____

_____

_____

Wave 3

+   —   Can you count five waves (three in the direction of the trend, two corrective)?

+   —   Do the two corrective waves show alternation?

+   —   Is the alternation in the form of price?

+   —   Is the alternation in the form of wave structure?

+   —   Is the alternation in the form of time?

        At this point, check for Fibonacci time ratios between the first and second correction.

+   —   Are there any Fibonacci time ratios between correction 1 and correction 2?

+   —   When comparing the three waves that move in the direction of the new trend, is one of these waves longer than the other two?

+   −   When comparing the three waves that move in the direction of the new trend, is the middle wave longer in price than at least one of the other waves?

If the middle wave is the shortest, this move is a correction.

If you believe that you are in wave 3 and you can count only three waves before wave 4 enters the price area of wave 1, you are now in wave B of an irregular correction.

Comments: _____

_____

_____

_____

_____

_____

_____

_____

Wave 4

+   −   Can you count three waves only in wave A?

+   −   Can you count three waves only in wave B?

+   −   Can you count either three or five waves in wave C?

+   −   Wave 4 can be a five wave triangle. If so, are all five legs made up of three waves, not five?

Wave 4 can often take up much more time and be far more complex than wave 2. As an indicator that wave 4 is complete, use Fibonacci time ratios.

+   –   When you compare the time that wave 2 took to complete, does wave 4 relate by any Fibonacci ratio (such as, 61.8 percent, 161.8 percent, 238.2 percent or 261.8 percent)?

+   –   Does wave 4 stay out of the price range of wave 1? If the answer is no, you are definitely in a correction.

Wave 4 can be shorter in time if wave 2 was unusually complex and time-consuming. In this case, wave 4 will often be a severe price correction and will be obvious when you look at your price charts.

+   –   Is there price alternation between wave 2 and wave 4?

+   –   Is there structure alternation between wave 2 and wave 4 (e.g., wave 2 may be a zigzag and wave 4 a flat)?

+   –   Is there time alternation between wave 2 and wave 4?

+   –   Has a contracting triangle completed?

At this point, be prepared to take any entry signal in the direction of the trend.

Comments: _____

_____

_____

_____

_____

_____

_____

_____

Wave 5

+   –   Can you count five waves (three in the direction of the trend, two corrective)?

+   –   Do the two corrective waves show alternation?

+   –   Is the alternation in the form of price?

+   –   Is the alternation in the form of wave structure?

+   –   Is the alternation in the form of time?

            Also at this point, check for Fibonacci time ratios between the first and second corrections.

+   –   Are there any Fibonacci time rations between correction 1 and correction 2?

+   –   When comparing the three waves that move in the direction of the trend, is one of these waves longer than the other two?

+   –   When comparing the three waves that move in the direction of the new trend, is the middle wave longer in price than at least one of the other waves?

            If the middle wave is the shortest, this move is a correction.

            If you believe that you are in wave 5 and you can count only three waves before wave 4 enters the price area of wave 1, you are still in a correction.

            Comments: _____

_____

_____

_____

_____

_____

_____

Wave 5 Triangle

If wave 4 has obviously completed but the next move in the direction of the trend is corrective, you have a good case that a triangle top is forming. Wave 1 will at first appear impulsive; but when you look closer to its structure, you will find that it is actually corrective.

Is there a lack of alternation between the two corrective waves that make up wave 1 in the following ways?

+   −   Time

+   −   Price

+   −   Structure

+   −   Is the third wave of wave 1 the shortest of the three waves? (This is not essential.)

+   −   Can you deduce from the above answers that wave 1 is corrective? In this case, relabel wave 1 as wave A.

+   −   Does wave 2 subdivide into three waves only? If so, label this as wave B.

+   −   Does wave 3 subdivide into three waves only? If so, label this as wave C.

+   −   Does wave 4 subdivide into three waves only? If so, label this as wave D.

               Do the price ranges of wave B, wave C and wave D overlap?

+   −   Does wave 5 subdivide into three waves only? If so, label this as wave E.

+   −   Sometimes wave 5 will appear impulsive and will make new market highs, but on closer inspection wave 5 will be corrective.

               Is there lack of alternation between the two corrective waves that make up wave 5 in the following ways?

+   −   Time

+   −   Price

+   –   Structure

+   –   Is the third wave of wave 1 the shortest of the three waves? (This in not essential.)

+   –   Can you deduce from the above answers that wave 5 is corrective? In this case, relabel wave 5 as wave E.

At this point, draw a trendline linking waves B and D. When this trendline is broken, the wave 5 triangle is complete.

Place an entry stop underneath/above the start of wave d with a protective stop loss above/below the high/low. The market will now begin a change of trend or enter a major corrective period. Its price strength and duration will depend on the degree of the waves that you have been analyzing.

Index